THE AUDACIOUS RISE OF KCPT

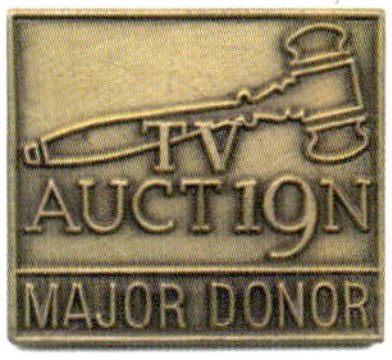

THE AUDACIOUS RISE OF KCPT

50 Years of Daring Broadcasting at Kansas City's Public Television Station

By Edward T. Matheny, Jr.

Foreword by C. W. Gusewelle

Published by Kansas City Star Books
1729 Grand Blvd.
Kansas City, MO 64108

Published by Kansas City Star Books
1729 Grand Boulevard
Kansas City, Missouri 64108
Kansascity.com

First Edition, First Printing

ISBN: 9781611690491
Library of Congress Control Number: 2012937129

Editor and project manager:
Carol Powers

Book designer:
DJ Hyde Matheny, the ping pong studio

Printed in the United States of America
by Walsworth Publishing Co., Inc., Marceline, Mo.

To order copies, call StarInfo, 816-234-4636 (say "operator").
Or go to www.TheKansasCityStore.com

KANSAS CITY STAR BOOKS

I WAS JUST OUT OF HARVARD Law School when I went to work at Caldwell, Downing, Noble & Garrity (now, several mergers later, Husch Blackwell), and have been here in one capacity or another ever since. One of the firm's clients was the School District of Kansas City, Missouri. It remains a client to this day — at 95 years, the oldest.

The attorney-client relationship provided an opportunity for me to be a repository of obscure incidents in our community's history, and an occasional minor participant.

One example: why is the street wider in front of the Board of Education building at 311 E. 12th?

When that building was built, Mayor H. Roe Bartle of Boy Scout fame and his City Council saw an opportunity to relieve some traffic congestion and offered the School District a considerable sum of money for a strip of land fronting on the building. The offer was accepted and the street widened accordingly, but the purchase price went unpaid. And so, year after year, on the 4th of July, the School Board secretary, dignified Amos Burks, set up saw horses in the street to assert dominion over the land in question. Finally, Mayor Ilus (Ike) Davis, wanting to end what he regarded as an embarrassing standoff, proposed to me that in exchange for a clear title certain city services be provided free of charge. The School Board agreed and the matter was laid to rest peaceably.

KCPT was another opportunity. Our law firm was involved in 1961 when the School District and its foresighted superintendent James Hazlett obtained a license and began to broadcast instructional television into class rooms. I was legal counsel for the District when the School Board and Hazlett concluded that a community-owned station would better serve the metropolitan area, and I became a part of that enterprise. My initial colleagues were visionaries who contributed essential resources to what would become one of the country's very best public television stations.

These founders deserve to be remembered, as do those who came after them. This history is a tribute to them, their successors, and the talented, dedicated professionals that KCPT has managed to attract and retain over the past half century.

— Edward T. Matheny, Jr.

The classic Indian Chief TV test pattern was used until well into the 1960's to adjust the studio cameras. That involved comparing the camera's image of the test pattern with a signal of the test pattern etched onto a cathode ray tube. The elements of the test pattern weren't just decorative: The chief was shaded to get contrast and brightness correct. The "pincushions" in the corners were to get the image square and filling the screen. Depending on your station, the test pattern usually came on right after midnight as regular programming went off, right after the "The Star Spangled Banner." Usually, it was accompanied by a head-splitting test tone.

HOW WE GOT THE 'TUBE'

TELEVISION, by most accounts, was born in 1936 when the British Broadcasting Company began transmitting from the Victorian Alexandra Palace in north London. A year later, on Armistice Day 1937, the BBC broadcast the first live street scene, allowing the public to watch on a television set as King George VI laid a wreath at the war memorial, the Cenotaph.

In 1939, standing on the shoulders of American television pioneer Philo Farnsworth, the Radio Corporation of America (RCA) televised the opening of the New York World's Fair , including a speech by President Franklin Delano Roosevelt.

That year, in Kansas City, Steve Melcher was introduced to television at a birthday party at Ricky Smalley's house. Steve remembers it this way:

I was in Ricky Smalley's kindergarten class. In the spring of 1939, Ricky had a birthday party to which I was invited. While the other boys played Pin the Tail on the Donkey, I sat mesmerized in front of this wooden console with a round eye and some knobs.

Mrs. Smalley came over to me and gently urged me to join the other boys. I said OK, but first I wanted to know what this console was. She said it was a television, but that we had no stations yet. She turned on the Indian Chief test pattern for me. I'd heard of television but had never seen one up close.

My dad, Darius Melcher of Butler Manufacturing, always wanted to be first where electronics were concerned, so the next day a television arrived at our house. Just to hedge his bets, my dad had a record player in the console in case TV didn't make it. I have often wondered what influence Ricky's father had on Dad and the purchase of that TV. Obviously, Ricky's dad was out in front of things from very early in life.

(Ricky Smalley, later Dr. Richard Smalley, would graduate from Kansas City's Southwest High School in 1961 and in 1996 be awarded the Nobel Prize in Chemistry.)

Developing the new medium of television was delayed by World War II, as war production took priority over everything else. TV broadcasting resumed in earnest in 1947, the year that a freckle-faced boy marionette named "Howdy Doody" debuted, to the delight of children. By 1949, American viewers had their choice of two 15-minute newscasts: "CBS-TV News" with Douglas Edwards and NBC's "The Camel News Caravan" with John Cameron Swayze. ABC News also had begun regular broadcasts. There were about a million TV sets in American homes.

By the early 1950s, 12 million Americans had television sets. "The Jack Benny Program," "Amos 'n' Andy" and "Kukla, Fran and Ollie" had begun.

In 1953, the Kansas City, Missouri, School District began to explore the possibility that local commercial stations could air educational programming — for example, home economics programs and science experiments. In 1957, the district broadcast a fifth-grade geography series, "Geography of Asia," on KMBC-TV Channel 5.

Within a short time, each of Kansas City's commercial TV stations was furnishing 30 minutes a day, five days a week, of educational programming, greatly impressing Superintendent James A. Hazlett with the usefulness of instructional television.

There's no way he could have foreseen "Sesame Street." But we can make that trip.

1960
John F. Kennedy is elected president. A pre-election televised debate with his opponent Richard M. Nixon has contrasted, for many, Nixon's poor television presence with Kennedy's poise.

1963
Most Americans watch TV for coverage of the shocking assassination of President Kennedy and the aftermath.

60

1962
The "CBS Evening News with Walter Cronkite introduces viewing audiences to the journalist who later will top public opinion surveys as "the most trusted man in America."

1964
Color comes to prime-time broadcasting.

HOW CLASSROOM TV BEGAT BIG BIRD

1961–1971

IT WAS A DECADE IN WHICH AMERICANS GREW INCREASINGLY FASCINATED WITH TELEVISION. THE MEDIUM'S PALETTE CHANGED FROM SHADES OF GRAY TO FULL COLOR. THERE WERE THREE MAJOR NETWORKS. BUT IN 1967, A GAME-CHANGING NATIONAL REPORT RECOMMENDED THE CREATION OF A FOURTH — A NONCOMMERCIAL *PUBLIC* TELEVISION NETWORK. IN KANSAS CITY, A SMALL GROUP OF CIVIC LEADERS WERE ENTHUSIASTICALLY ON BOARD WITH THE IDEA, AND THEY PUT THEIR BACKS, REPUTATIONS AND SOME PERSONAL MONIES INTO THE TASK OF MAKING IT HAPPEN. THE PRECURSOR OF WHAT WOULD BECOME A VITAL PUBLIC STATION CAME TO THEIR ATTENTION. ITS CALL LETTERS WERE KCSD.

1965 Coverage of the Vietnam War gives many Americans their first realistic look at the horrors of combat.

1967 There are three major networks, CBS, NBC and ABC. The Carnegie Commission recommends creation of a fourth, a public television network.

1968 Dr. Martin Luther King Jr. is assassinated April 4 in Memphis, Tenn., and U.S. Senator Robert F. Kennedy is slain June 5 in Los Angeles.

1971 CBS's "All in the Family" heralds the arrival of more realistic situation comedies. Daytime TV still is mostly soap operas and quiz shows.

71

If it weren't for Philo T. Farnsworth, inventor of television, we'd still be eating frozen radio dinners.
– JOHNNY CARSON

Superintendent of Schools James A. Hazlett immediately saw the promise of instructional television.

KANSAS CITY educators were so sold on the promise of television that when a new school administration building was constructed at 1211 McGee St., it was designed to accommodate modern television production facilities on the 11th floor. The transmitter was located on the 23rd floor of City Hall. Given that some channels were being designated "educational," the school district applied for and was assigned a license for Channel 19. It would be an ultrahigh frequency (UHF) channel, with the call letters KCSD.

On March 29, 1961, KCSD-TV telecast its first instructional program, in which Superintendent James Hazlett addressed students and teachers by means of the new medium. Among his comments was an endorsement: "We now have the equipment and physical facilities to provide a powerful educational influence in metropolitan Kansas City."

Because most home television sets were equipped to receive only VHF (very high frequency) channels, KCSD's UHF programs were initially the best kept secret in town. That lasted until the All Channels Receiver Act in 1962 required that all TV sets manufactured after 1964 be equipped to transmit both VHF and UHF channels. Also in 1962, a federal grant paid for increased power that extended KCSD's range to 38 air miles — as distant as Raytown, Parkville and Independence in Missouri, and even Leavenworth, Kan. Daytime programming increased from 27 to 47 live telecasts in just a few months.

Even though most television households still had only VHF reception, the future was evident. An advertisement for converters in the *Kansas City Kansan* newspaper explained that when KCSD began prime evening telecasts on Feb. 6, 1962, only VHF viewers with "the necessary converting apparatus attached to your set" would be able to receive the UHF signal.

Zoel Parenteau was KCSD's first station manager. In a later article in *KCPT Magazine*, he recalled that KCSD's first 15-minute classroom telecasts were specifically designed to complement the Kansas City School District's curriculum. Television teachers' topics focused on subjects that were difficult to staff in the classroom, such as Spanish and science. The four original on-air teachers, Carlotta Cumming, MinaRuth Galey, Lillian DaKopollus, and Geraldine Workman, were soon joined by a fifth, Frank Guemple.

(Continued on page 7)

Zoel Parenteau, KCSD's first station manager, at the controls in the Board of Education Building. Partly obscured is long-time KCSD chief engineer Clyde Howe.

A TV teacher does a live telecast in the early 1960s.

(Continued from page 4)

TEACHERS ON THE TUBE

In 1964, Mrs. Barton Cohen became a KCSD television teacher. She had a master's degree in science education for elementary teachers from New York's Columbia University, and was assigned to teach science on television for grades K-7 even though she had never seen a TV camera. It proved to be a very good fit.

There were hazards. Studio support was rudimentary: Flip cards served as teleprompters and teachers provided their own props, usually pictures they cut from magazines.

The telecasts were live — warts and all, with no retakes in case of errors or omissions or catastrophes. Mary Davidson Cohen's first live telecast, an experiment for a fourth-grade "Air and Water" class, resulted in water leaking all over her notes, making the green ink indecipherable, but she persevered and completed the experiment. Her favorite course was "Farm Animals," for kindergarteners.

A friendly farmer delivered baby goats to the station, which she bottle-fed on camera. Likewise with baby pigs. Mary composed a ditty for the students to sing in their classrooms, following her studio warbling. It began: "I go to the farm and what do I see? The cow and chickens are lookin' at me..."

Mary Cohen's pioneer TV teaching career at KCSD ended with the birth of her son in January 1966, but it is an experience she recalls with great affection. She obtained her doctorate in education administration in 1977 and in 2002 was appointed regional representative for the U.S. Secretary of Education. She has maintained her support for Channel 19 as executive director of the Barton P. and Mary D. Cohen Charitable Trust.

Early television could have used funding from the Cohen trust. In 1966, after a year-long study commissioned by the powerful philanthropic Carnegie Corporation, the Carnegie Commission on Educational Television issued a strongly positive report, "Public Television: *A Program for Action.*"

One of its recommendations was that this expensive new public television business should be funded by a manufacturers' excise tax on all television sets. That would have funded the new medium comparably to what England then provided to its public broadcasting service.

To promote the development of non-commercial TV, the act also established the Corporation for Public Broadcasting (CPB). One of its jobs would be to garner

TV teachers' 15-minute telecasts complemented classroom lessons.

A Carnegie Corporation report on educational TV was strongly positive.

University of Kansas City Chancellor Emeritus Carleton F. Scofield believed KCSD could become a real community station.

Homer Wadsworth, president and executive director of the Kansas City Association of Trusts and Foundations, financed Scofield's report.

federal subsidies for educational TV stations — although the amounts appropriated would never be enough. Without adequate government funding and with FCC restrictions on commercial advertising on public TV, the stations were left to themselves to figure out how to raise money for their yearly budgets.

Gradually, the TV that came into being as "educational television" began to call itself "public television," a term coined by the Carnegie Commission. It was not a replacement for educational television, but a subdivision. In 1967 KCSD took the cue, broadening its mission beyond classroom programming but still devoting its schedule in large measure to formal instruction.

FIRST STUDIO TELECAST, THE FIRST PUNDITS?

On Jan. 6, 1971, "Your Congressman," a weekly half-hour show with Missouri House Rules Committee Chairman Richard Bolling, debuted as Channel 19's first in studio telecast. The prominent Democratic legislator's first guest was a former Labor Department official. In the weeks to come, guests included the legislative representative of the International Ladies Garment Union, and William Clay, Missouri's first black Congressman. The program was replaced later by a broad-based public affairs production, "Kansas City Looks at Washington," with Bolling and others presenting viewpoints on issues of current interest on Capitol Hill. The first of these telecasts was from Washington and dealt with health insurance.

Elsewhere in the country, TV stations originally licensed by school districts were beginning to realize that their real calling might be bringing public television to the entire community. In Kansas City, Superintendent Hazlett was coming to that conclusion, with the encouragement of Carleton F. Scofield, chancellor emeritus of the University of Kansas City, and Homer Wadsworth, president and executive director of the Kansas City Association of Trusts and Foundations.

In August 1968, Dr. Scofield had submitted a report he prepared on public television, financed by Wadsworth's Association. Because I was serving as legal counsel for the Kansas City School District, Hazlett forwarded the report to me, calling it "a basis for planning ways by which KCSD-TV can become a meaningful public television station."

We all knew the school district was limited in tax money it could spend for public television. But as Hazlett noted, in KCSD we had a public resource with untapped potential. The obvious problem: How can we afford to make this resource available to the larger community?

(Continued on page 10)

THE NEW YORK TIMES, SUNDAY, JANUARY 29, 1967.

The New York Times.

Published every day by The New York Times Company

ADOLPH S. OCHS, *Publisher 1896-1935*
ORVIL E. DRYFOOS, *Publisher 1961-1963*

ALL THE NEWS THAT'S FIT TO PRINT
ESTABLISHED 1851

ARTHUR HAYS SULZBERGER
Chairman of the Board
ARTHUR OCHS SULZBERGER
President and Publisher

HARDING F. BANCROFT, *Executive Vice President*
ANDREW FISHER, *Vice President*
MONROE GREEN, *Vice President*
IVAN VEIT, *Vice President*
FRANCIS A. COX, *Secretary-Treasurer*

TURNER CATLEDGE, *Executive Editor*
JOHN B. OAKES, *Editorial Page Editor*

LESTER MARKEL, *Associate Editor*
JAMES RESTON, *Associate Editor*

A Civilized Voice for TV

"Public television is capable of becoming the clearest expression of American diversity, and of excellence within diversity." That is the glowing vision the long-awaited report of the Carnegie Commission on Educational Television holds out to a nation accustomed to banality on the home screen.

Without derogating the services of commercial television, the report takes realistic note of the medium's dependence on sponsor support and the effect in reducing many of its programs to the lowest common denominator of audience interest. The very effort to satisfy as broad an audience as possible makes the networks an additional force for conformity in a conformist society. Noncommercial television, in the words of E. B. White, should address itself to "the ideal of excellence, not the idea of acceptability —which is what keeps commercial television from climbing the staircase."

The Carnegie Commission report shares the spirit of the Ford Foundation's far-reaching proposals last summer for a "people's dividend" to finance educational TV, but it presents a sounder basic approach to underwriting and organizing the new system. Instead of depending on savings in communications costs made possible by a new domestic satellite system—a source at once inadequate and difficult to defend—the Carnegie report proposes a relatively modest excise tax on all new television sets. That is a logical place to get the money; but the commission stresses that it is not wedded to that source if Congress prefers to tap another it considers more equitable.

The panel's real concern is to assure a dependable and self-renewing supply of public funds to shield the new system from the political pressures that would be inescapable if it had to go to Congress for fresh appropriations each year.

The commission provides impressive support for its conviction that an independent and comprehensive educational TV system will affect American tastes and standards in ways that will stimulate both the old and the new networks to more daring, more diversified and more significant activity in the public interest.

The Columbia Broadcasting System's initial gift of a million dollars to help bring into being the proposed Corporation for Public Television reflects a healthy recognition that there is strength for all TV in this broadening of the medium's usefulness. Dr. James R. Killian Jr. and his associates in the commission have made a major contribution to public understanding; now it is up to President Johnson and Congress to proceed with a program to realize TV's potential, along the broad lines of the Carnegie report.

Above, a New York Times editorial endorsed the Carnegie Commission's belief in the potential of public television.

Below, "Your Congressman" Richard Bolling talks with Ladies Garment Workers Union representative Evelyn Dubrow in KCSD's first in-studio telecast.

Tell It To Your Congressman

KANSAS CITY'S Congressman Richard Bolling and Miss Evelyn Dubrow, Legislative Representative of the International Ladies Garment Workers Union, recently discussed consumer legislation passed by the Congress on KCSD-TV. The program was aired Jan. 4. Miss Dubrow, who is a member of the Consumers Federation of America, largest consumer group in the country, credited Mr. Bolling and the Rules Committee of which he is a member for speeding up enactment of the bill in the House which sets up an independent Consumer Protection Agency.

"Mr. Rogers' Neighborhood" had a trolley ...

... and a school bus

... and a King Friday puppet.

COURTESY OF THE FRED ROGERS COMPANY AND ©THE FRED ROGERS COMPANY

(Continued from page 8)

Considering much the same question, the Carnegie Commission report had recommended the creation of a public television network. The Corporation for Public Broadcasting wasn't authorized to handle that role. So, at the urging of noncommercial station managers, the Public Broadcasting System (PBS) was created to look after programming on a nationwide basis. PBS would not produce its own programs — that was to be done largely by individual PBS stations and shared with other PBS members.

A FINE FEATHERED FRIEND

Public television always considered children a primary audience. In the late 1960s, it became a petri dish for cultivating wildly creative children's programming. The shows developed by PBS stations caught most everyone (parents, early childhood education experts and TV critics) by surprise.

A harbinger, "Mr. Rogers' Neighborhood" made its national debut on public television in 1968. Fred Rogers, described as "the Pied Piper of Television," was an ordained Presbyterian minister whose ministry was work with children through television. Fond of sneakers and sweaters, he was laid back, almost laconic, and talked directly to the camera because, as he said, "kids can spot a phony a mile away." His program was intended for preschoolers and, later studies showed, had a big effect on their learning readiness.

"Sesame Street" — a program in which startling puppets and a few humans educated young viewers in a way no book or teacher could — made its Channel 19 debut on the morning of Nov. 10, 1969. Childhood would never be the same.

The KCSD Program Guide introduced it as "an hour-long adventure in fun and learning for the pre-school youngster." The producer was the Children's Television Workshop, funded primarily by the U.S. Office of Education, CPB, and the Ford and Carnegie foundations.

Anchoring the show was a giant canary named Big Bird, invented by the late Jim Henson, creator of the Muppets, and the late costume maker, Kermit Love. Caroll Spinney, the man still inside the bird, has spent half his life in a bird costume.

"Sesame Street" was in its infancy when Henson hired Spinney to play two characters he was developing for the show — Big Bird, and Oscar the Grouch, who lived in a trash can. In his book, *The Wisdom of Big Bird (and the Dark Genius of Oscar the Grouch)*, Spinney said he knew at the outset that Big Bird was a big deal, but had no idea how big he would become.

Educational television should be absolutely forbidden.
It can only lead to unreasonable disappointment when your child discovers that
the letters of the alphabet do not leap up and dance around with royal-blue chickens.
– FRAN LEBOWITZ

Big Bird dropped by a Channel 19 event.

Big Bird and Oscar the Grouch on later KCPT Magazine covers ...

... and the 1971 cover of KCSD's program guide.

The large yellow avian was designed with the personality and skill set of the average 6-year-old. Sure enough, young viewers came to identify with and love him, despite his bizarre appearance and towering height.

Of course Big Bird and the other denizens of "Sesame Street" weren't just a vehicle for teaching the alphabet and other fundamentals, but social values as well. (One of Ernie's songs was "Don't Throw That Trash on the Ground.") Life was tough on the street. Consider the decision to take on the death of beloved character Mr. Hooper. Why did he die? In addition to cheering up education, "Sesame Street," in the words of geek-favorite writer Garth Sundem, "mirrored young viewers' own complex, deeply felt lives." Big Bird and Oscar were joined by such characters as Bert and Ernie, Count von Count, Cookie Monster, Mr. Snuffleupagus and Grover and Elmo, all sprung from the genius of Jim Henson.

(Continued on page 14)

A young viewer sent in his drawing of "Sesame Street's" Cookie Monster in his Cookie Van.

COOKIE
van

"The Electric Company" was introduced by the Children's Television Workshop after "Sesame Street" and taught reading skills to older children.

Reminders of the popularity of "Sesame Street" were everywhere.

(Continued from page 11)

In 1971, the Children's Television Workshop introduced "The Electric Company," with similar success. Featuring Morgan Freeman and Rita Moreno, it was a "Sesame Street" companion piece for slightly older youngsters, designed to teach basic skills to those experiencing reading difficulties.

One of those captivated by "Sesame Street" was a grandson of George E. Powell Sr., honorary chairman emeritus of Yellow Freight Systems. Powell was struck by his grandson's response to Big Bird. George E. Powell III remembers the time:

> *My clearest memory was listening to my grandfather talk about "Sesame Street." One day he observed one of my younger cousins watching Big Bird on the show. It was the FIrst time he became aware of the program. He was impressed by how fascinated my cousin was and quickly recognized how valuable television could be in educating young children.*
>
> *He also, however, was skeptical about the interest that commercial television would have in participating. He said that was what motivated him to be part of securing a future for public television in Kansas City.*

"Sesame Street" was broadcast live each weekday morning on Channel 19, but had to be recorded for playback if there were to be afternoon shows. Underwriting grants paid for the afternoon telecasts. The Kansas City chapter of the American Institute of Architects presented a check to KCSD for the first of these grants, underwriting afternoon broadcasts from Nov. 11 to Dec. 31, 1969.

The Ford Foundation had been educational television's single biggest benefactor, and one of its contributions was the Station Independence Project (SIP). SIP sought ways to raise money for penniless public television, and from this came the popular culture staple: pledge drives. In October 1970, still under the auspices of KCSD, Channel 19 conducted its first pledge drive, a week long effort. As the November 1970 KCSD Program Guide reported:

> *Pledge week was a new experience for our staff as well as our viewers, and we all gained a great deal of knowledge about how to conduct it (and how not to conduct it). We want to give special thanks to the Kansas City Junior League for providing volunteer operators through their provisional program for all six nights. Our membership pledges totaled slightly more than $4,000."*

Mrs. J. L. Weinberg, center, and Mrs. Frank Meyer, president and vice president of the Kansas City section of the National Council of Jewish Women, gave a check for $1,000 to Zoel Parenteau to keep afternoon telecasts of "Sesame Street" on the air.

Speakers Bureau volunteers have a planning meeting.

Nowlin Hall senior volunteers sort instructional TV materials.

Prospective Friends of TV 19 attend an orientation meeting.

A grant to KCSD from the Greater Kansas City Section of the National Council of Jewish Women paid for continuation of the Sesame Street broadcasts in 1970.

But financing to keep the afternoon broadcasts going was tenuous. The February 1971 KCSD Program Guide revealed that the American Federation of Teachers was a benefactor with an extension through the 23rd of the month. A March 1971 edition of *The Kansas City Times* reported that a $46 gift from students at Swinney Elementary School had bought a day's reprieve for Big Bird after funds ran out. Other spasmodic funders included First National Bank, the Kansas City Chapter of Jack and Jill, Benton Auto Parts Company, and the Kansas City Association of Trusts and Foundations. These cliffhangers continued for Big Bird until the *The Kansas City Star* and *Times* began underwriting the show on a regular basis.

Clearly, there was need to inform the public of what PBS offered, and how a community television station raises the money necessary to keep going and growing. An invitation for membership in something called "Members of 19" was broadcast in October 1969. And there were supportive editorials on KCMO-TV and WDAF-TV.

Meanwhile, there were efforts to create a different structure for Channel 19. The Kansas City School Board went on record as favoring the eventual withdrawal of the school district from the field of public television. In response, Community Service Broadcasting of Mid-America, Inc. (CSB) was incorporated in November 1970 to support public television in the Kansas City metropolitan area, and specifically Channel 19.

DEEP CUT IN SCHOOL BUDGET

Board Pares 3.3 Million Dollars Off 1969-70 Spending by Eliminating 255 Teaching Positions and Curtailing Programs, Including Subsidy of Lunches

RAISES INTACT

Teachers to Start at $6,-600 as Earlier Approved

CLASS SIZE MAY RISE

Teacher Agent Will Oppose Any Load Increases

By Patricia Jansen Doyle
(The Star's Education Editor)

The Kansas City Board of Education sliced 3.3 million dollars yesterday from its budget for the 1969-70 year, including the elimination of about 255 teaching positions which existed last year.

In the unanimous action the six board members also reaffirmed salary increases approved conditionally in February. It was noted that the new beginning teacher salary of $6,600 was needed to keep Kansas City competitive with other school districts in this region.

James A. Hazlett, superintendent of schools, said eliminating the 255 teaching jobs would save the district $2,040,000

AMID DEBATE ON reducing educational staff and programs in the Kansas City school district, James A. Hazlett, superintendent, scratched his head while Mrs. Tom J. Stubbs, board president, listened solemnly to views of a colleague—(Kansas City Star photograph by K. Kenneth

WILL BUS MORE

Board Votes to Transport 800 Manual Students

TO USE M'GEE BUILDING

Second Technical Education Center Pact Awarded

By Peg McMahon
(A Member of The Star's Staff)

Eight hundred Manual students will be bussed to classes in the former junior college building at 3845 McGee street, beginning in September, the Kansas City Board of Education said yesterday.

The unanimous board action was taken because construction of the city-wide Technical Education Center, now under way on the Manual site, will necessitate razing the academic section of the Manual building when the construction strike ends.

The board also awarded contracts totaling $2,153,645 for the second phase of construction on the Technical Education Center on the Manual site. The awards were made on the basis of firm bids received in September.

Drastic school budget cuts eliminated district funding for programs like instructional TV.

(Continued from page 17)

The birth of CSB came just in the nick of time. The Kansas City School District had been compelled to cut its public television support in half. A television teacher such as Mary Cohen was a thing of the past. The District needed to seek funding from the community at large in 1971 in order to continue any instructional TV. This was a daunting task because Missouri's school finance laws required school levies and bond issues to pass by a two-thirds vote. From 1969 to 1987, the district was never successful in passing a measure of either sort, despite 19 attempts.

In February, more directors were added, including Dr. James C. Olson, chancellor of the University of Missouri-Kansas City, and Kansas City, Kans., Mayor Joseph McDowell. An instructional television committee was appointed, led by Dr. Arzell Ball, superintendent of schools for the up-and-coming Shawnee Mission School District.

KCSD's instructional TV programs had been broadcast to various school districts in the metropolitan area, and no one thought this would change when the license transferred to CSB. CSB received its first donations, shares of stock from CSB director Louis Sosland, General Manager of Sosland Brothers, and stock in Businessmen's Assurance Company (BMA) from that company's honorary chairman, J.C. Higdon. (William Grant, BMA chairman and president, was a member of the CSB Board.)

Lights, Camera, Action!

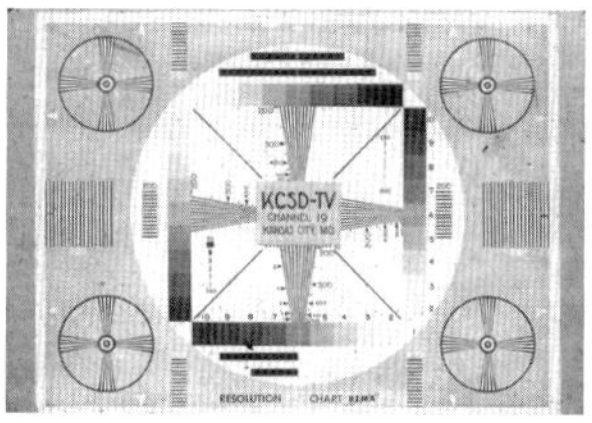

The KCSD Test Pattern

Dr. James C. Olson, chancellor of the University of Missouri-Kansas City

Joseph McDowell, mayor of Kansas City, Kansas

CSB director Louis Sosland, general manager of Sosland Brothers

J. C. Higdon, Businessmen's Assurance Company honorary chairman

On May 20, 1971, the IRS issued a determination letter ruling that CSB was a tax-exempt 501(c)(3) organization and that contributions, bequests and other gifts were tax deductible by donors.

In August, a contract between the School District and CSB provided for CSB to succeed the District as licensee of Channel 19. CSB was to "use its best efforts to provide a new physical plant for use by the station, including a transmitter site and tower, together with a five-fold increase of power and conversion to color broadcasting." The station was to be operated as a nonprofit, noncommercial television broadcast station.

Under the contract, CSB would make its broadcast facilities available between certain hours Monday through Friday for instructional TV programs but only if the participating school districts defrayed the cost.

Application for transfer of the Channel 19 license was filed in October, and Zoel Parenteau informed the general public of this in an announcement on Channel 19.

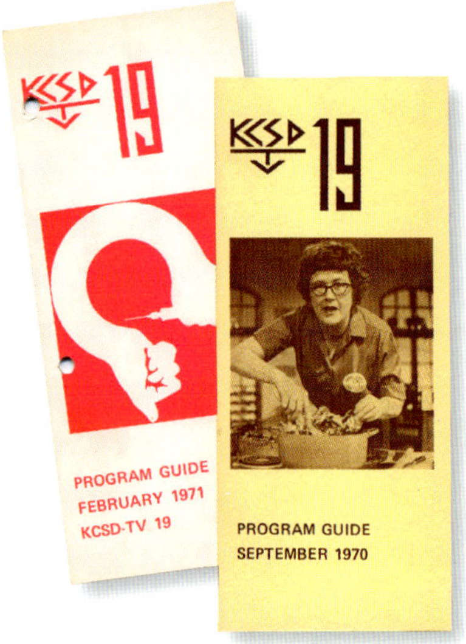

Program guides spotlight a documentary on drug abuse and Julia Child's program.

A TIMELY BANKRUPTCY

Then we learned of the bankruptcy of Allied Broadcasting Company, which operated KCIT-TV, a commercial television station at 2100 Stark Ave. in unincorporated Blue Summit, Mo. I attended a hearing on the matter at the courthouse in Kansas City, and later presented the facts and figures to the CSB Board. Allied's assets were to be sold in three "packages": real estate including studio and office building, a mobile trailer, and personal property. The indispensable tower and transmitter, owned by RCA, would be handled in a separate transaction.

Homer Wadsworth told the board that two of its members had agreed to personally guarantee a bank loan to pay for the real and personal property, and 75 percent of the cost of the tower and transmitter could be defrayed through a Health, Education and Welfare Department grant. Buying these properties would go a long way toward satisfying the commitment to the school district to "provide a new physical plant for use by the station."

A March 1971 cover features the much-examined show "The Great American Dream Machine."

George Powell, Carleton Scofield and James Olson all insisted that CSB had an opportunity it could not afford to miss. The board authorized the executive committee to take the necessary steps to purchase the Allied assets and to deal with RCA for the purchase of tower and transmitter. The committee also was authorized to negotiate loans for the purchases with First National Bank.

On October 29, 1971, the Allied real estate package was offered for sale to the highest bidder in an auction in Room 927 in the U.S. Courthouse. The CSB executive committee was there. The auctioneer, Darold W. Jenkins, had been an All-American center on the University of Missouri football team and clearly

(Continued on page 22)

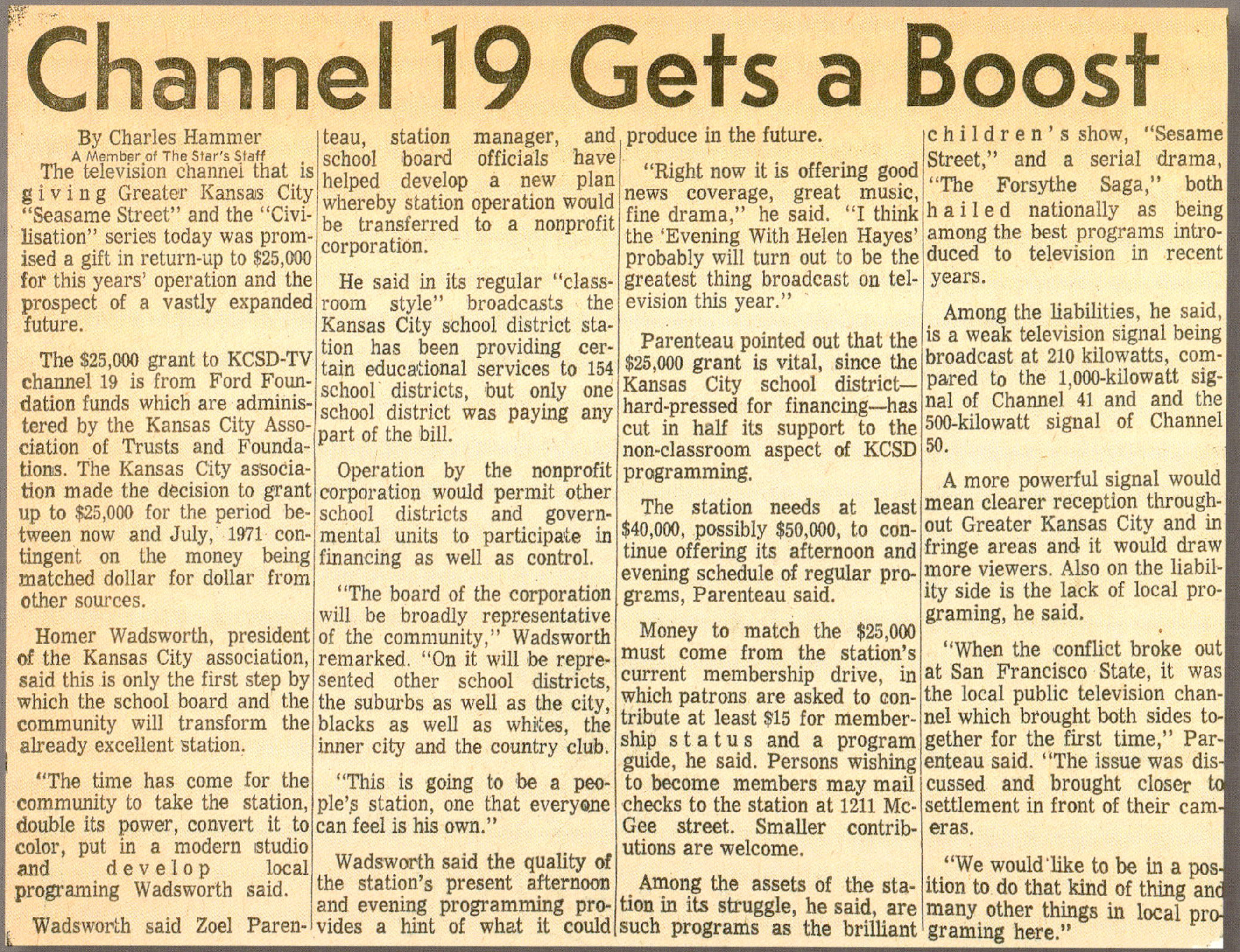

Channel 19 Gets a Boost

By Charles Hammer
A Member of The Star's Staff

The television channel that is giving Greater Kansas City "Seasame Street" and the "Civilisation" series today was promised a gift in return-up to $25,000 for this years' operation and the prospect of a vastly expanded future.

The $25,000 grant to KCSD-TV channel 19 is from Ford Foundation funds which are administered by the Kansas City Association of Trusts and Foundations. The Kansas City association made the decision to grant up to $25,000 for the period between now and July, 1971 contingent on the money being matched dollar for dollar from other sources.

Homer Wadsworth, president of the Kansas City association, said this is only the first step by which the school board and the community will transform the already excellent station.

"The time has come for the community to take the station, double its power, convert it to color, put in a modern studio and develop local programing Wadsworth said.

Wadsworth said Zoel Parenteau, station manager, and school board officials have helped develop a new plan whereby station operation would be transferred to a nonprofit corporation.

He said in its regular "classroom style" broadcasts the Kansas City school district station has been providing certain educational services to 154 school districts, but only one school district was paying any part of the bill.

Operation by the nonprofit corporation would permit other school districts and governmental units to participate in financing as well as control.

"The board of the corporation will be broadly representative of the community," Wadsworth remarked. "On it will be represented other school districts, the suburbs as well as the city, blacks as well as whites, the inner city and the country club.

"This is going to be a people's station, one that everyone can feel is his own."

Wadsworth said the quality of the station's present afternoon and evening programming provides a hint of what it could produce in the future.

"Right now it is offering good news coverage, great music, fine drama," he said. "I think the 'Evening With Helen Hayes' probably will turn out to be the greatest thing broadcast on television this year."

Parenteau pointed out that the $25,000 grant is vital, since the Kansas City school district—hard-pressed for financing—has cut in half its support to the non-classroom aspect of KCSD programming.

The station needs at least $40,000, possibly $50,000, to continue offering its afternoon and evening schedule of regular programs, Parenteau said.

Money to match the $25,000 must come from the station's current membership drive, in which patrons are asked to contribute at least $15 for membership status and a program guide, he said. Persons wishing to become members may mail checks to the station at 1211 McGee street. Smaller contributions are welcome.

Among the assets of the station in its struggle, he said, are such programs as the brilliant children's show, "Sesame Street," and a serial drama, "The Forsythe Saga," both hailed nationally as being among the best programs introduced to television in recent years.

Among the liabilities, he said, is a weak television signal being broadcast at 210 kilowatts, compared to the 1,000-kilowatt signal of Channel 41 and and the 500-kilowatt signal of Channel 50.

A more powerful signal would mean clearer reception throughout Greater Kansas City and in fringe areas and it would draw more viewers. Also on the liability side is the lack of local programing, he said.

"When the conflict broke out at San Francisco State, it was the local public television channel which brought both sides together for the first time," Parenteau said. "The issue was discussed and brought closer to settlement in front of their cameras.

"We would like to be in a position to do that kind of thing and many other things in local programing here."

Star story reports a Ford Foundation grant of $25,000 to KCSD-TV.

While theoretically and technically television may be possible, commercially and financially I consider it an impossibility, a development of which we need waste little time dreaming.

– LEE DE FOREST,
American electrical and radio inventor

"Barket responded that he admired Homer Wadsworth and wanted him to have the station. Matheny replied: 'We are Homer Wadsworth.'"

(Continued from page 20)

enjoyed his role in the proceedings. The auction was described in a *Kansas City Times* article by Harry Jones Jr., headlined "Surprise Bids at KCIT Auction." Below are a few pertinent paragraphs from Jones' story:

> *Community Service Broadcasting of Mid-Americ a, Inc. (CSB) outbid Andrew (Skip) Carter, a radio station owner, for much of KCIT-TV, Channel 50, in an exciting public auction in federal bankruptcy court yesterday afternoon.*
>
> *The high bid, offered by Edward T. Matheny Jr., attorney for CSB, was $156,000. Involved in the purchase were 10 acres of land, the office and station building, the transmitter building and the concrete base of the tower.*
>
> *The auction at times was dramatic as Matheny and Carter, both seated in the audience of the packed courtroom, upped each other $1,000 at a time starting at $20,000.*
>
> *When Carter reached $141,000, a new bidder, Alex J. Barket, president of the Civic Plaza National Bank, entered the picture to the apparent surprise of both original bidders and to Darold W. Jenkins, receiver for the bankrupt television station who was serving as auctioneer.*
>
> *"I'll put in a bid for $145,000," Barket said from the back of the courtroom...*
>
> *Carter then bid $146,000 and Barket jumped him immediately to $150,000. Carter quickly went to $151,000. Barket paused, then offered $155,000.*
>
> *Jenkins had announced before the bidding that he would call a recess to give the bidders time to decide what to do once it appeared they had reached a high point. Barket's $155,000 bid signaled this recess...*
>
> *Matheny retired into another room with George E. Powell Sr., honorary chairman of the board of Yellow Freight Systems, Inc., Dr. Carleton F. Scofield, chancellor emeritus of the University of Missouri-Kansas City, and Michael F. Mayer, vice-president of the First National Bank of Kansas City. All are officers on the board of CSB.*

It will scramble up your head and drag your brain about.

– BOB DYLAN,
"TV Talking Song"

We had not intended to go above $150,000 but decided to go as high as $160,000. While we were discussing this, Barket entered the room and I asked him "Where did you come from?" Barket responded that he admired Homer Wadsworth and wanted him to have the station. I replied: "We are Homer Wadsworth."

The Times reporter wasn't privy to our recess exchange. His article continued with what occurred when the proceedings resumed:

> *Jenkins reopened the bidding and Matheny immediately topped Barket by $1,000 to $156,000... "I have no further bid," Carter replied....*
>
> *Asked why he had suddenly entered the bidding without having advised either Matheny or Carter of his interest in advance, Barket said he had read of the auction two days ago, and had noticed that Homer Wadsworth was a consultant to CSB. Since he had always admired Wadsworth he had decided to go to the auction and help CSB...*

Children's show host Torey Southwick became program manager at KCSD.

Whizzo the Clown was Southwick's crosstown rival.

CSB acquired 10 acres of land together with an office and trailer, studio building and transmitter building.

The diverse composition of the CSB board — 27 members at the time of the bankruptcy auction — reflected the broad community interest in public television. There also was continued interest on the part of the Kansas City School Board. The school district's contract with CSB required that the Kansas City superintendent of schools or his designee be on the CSB board as well as two school board appointees. To accommodate these additions, CSB enlarged the board to 30.

A Corporation for Public Broadcasting grant made it possible to hire popular children's show host Torey Southwick ("Torey Time," "Torey and Friends") as program manager at KCSD. Southwick was chosen from among 90 applicants by a joint committee of School District representatives and CSB. He brought an infusion of experience to the future Channel 19 licensee.

Torey and his puppet sidekick Ol' Gus had been hugely successful on KMBC-TV for nine years before moving to Channel 50 shortly before its demise. One 1967 ratings book for mornings when Torey was opposite "Today" and "Captain Kangaroo" placed his show higher than the other two combined. Equally well known was his crosstown rival Whizzo the Clown on KCMO-TV. (KCPT's Teddy Dibble would later produce the documentary "Whizzo, Old Gus and Me.")

Channel 19 bought the KCIT building in Blue Summit, near Independence, and the transmitter tower.

KCIT's antenna was removed to make way for Channel 19's transmitting equipment.

The control room at 2100 Stark in Blue Summit.

BY LATE OCTOBER 1971, Community Service Broadcasting of Mid-America (CSB) had bought the land, buildings and equipment of bankrupt TV station KCIT. The $156,000 purchase price was advanced by the First National Bank in return for two promissory notes – one secured by the property and the other by the personal guarantee of CSB directors George Powell and Louis Sosland.

The Federal Communications Commission approved the license transfer, and on Dec. 31, CSB took control of KCSD, Channel 19, from the school board.

The station's call letters were changed to KCPT.

On Jan. 7, 1972, KCPT staff began the move from 12th and Oak streets to the former KCIT studio building at 21st Street and Stark Avenue in Blue Summit.

CSB finalized a deal with RCA to buy the transmitter tower, its bargaining position enhanced by the tower's location on a base owned by CSB. Relocation of the tower would have been impractical, to say the least.

CSB negotiated with General Electric to buy a transmitter package that, along with some new studio equipment, would permit color broadcasts and a powerful signal throughout the entire metropolitan area. Department of Health, Education and Welfare funds came through and covered most of the cost of the transmitter.

On Jan. 28, there was a "housewarming" event at 21st and Stark, a fundraising luncheon "a la Julia Child."

George Powell reinforced his support of CSB in January 1972 with a substantial gift of Yellow Freight stock.

The same month, a new kind of children's series made its appearance on Channel 19. Unlike other children's fare, ZOOM was largely unscripted. It encouraged 8 to 12-year-olds to be active investigators, creators and problem-solvers in their lives – ironically, to "turn off the TV set." It usually had a cast of seven kids, called ZOOMers, who were known for wearing striped rugby shirts and jeans and performing barefoot. They did games, plays, poems, recipes, jokes, songs, science experiments and informal chats, all suggested by viewer write-ins.

In fact, KCPT had received an invitation in December from Boston public TV station WGBH, which produced the show, to submit material, written by children, for the program. The series would last six seasons and become famous for, among other things, its musical exhortation to: Write ZOOM, Z-Double-O-M, Box 3-5-0, Boston, Mass 0-2-1-3-4; send it to ZOOM!

(Continued on page 30)

The improvisational show, "ZOOM," and its ZOOMers, was aimed at 8 to 12-year-olds.

© DAVID WELSH

Wide-lens view of KCPT's new headquarters building at 2100 Stark.

The audio control room at 12th and Oak.

The master control room.

Camera control units.

An audio engineer.

Another KCSD engineer.

A film chain.

Robert Fuzy and auction volunteer Denny McWhinney.

McWhinney and Mary Toevs returned from San Francisco with plans for the first auction, above.

(Continued from page 26)

GOING ONCE, GOING TWICE ...

Also destined to become pervasive, a new fundraising vehicle called a TV auction was under consideration at Channel 19 in 1972.

San Francisco public television station KQED had conducted the first TV auction – in which celebrities auctioned off goods and services donated to the station – in 1955. Despite popularity in the bay area, KQED had been on the verge of bankruptcy and was rescued by the auction, which became an annual San Francisco event. Seeing KQED's success, other public TV stations followed suit.

Mrs. Rodney McWhinney and CSB second vice president Mrs. William F. Toevs were authorized in February to attend a Corporation for Public Broadcasting auction workshop in San Francisco. They returned from the auction workshop and, with Mrs. Michael Mayer, presented plans to the CSB board for an auction in the spring of 1973. Jacqueline Mayer, as Denny McWhinney's co-chair, would contribute much to the success that the auction later enjoyed.

Mary Toevs was part of a cadre of volunteers who were enthusiastic, valuable supporters of Channel 19. The chairwoman of volunteers for the station was Sarah Rowland, and it was her job to recruit, train and supply volunteers to the station as needed. Toevs brought a unique perspective because she also was on the board and executive committee of a national public broadcasting volunteers organization.

In April, Channel 19 got its first check from the cultural community when the Kansas City Civic Ballet Association requested a half hour of TV time during its Ballet Festival. The program began with an 18-minute film followed by a 10-minute discussion of the festival by three participants. The modest cost, $129.40, was covered by the Ballet Association.

More than 500 KCPT members responded to a questionnaire asking them to name the most needed TV program in Kansas City. The top vote-getter, according to general manager Zoel Parenteau, was local affairs.

In March 1972, KCPT tapped *The Kansas City Star's* education editor, Patricia Jansen Doyle, to help develop the station's Instructional TV (ITV) program. While the school district had discontinued the business of producing classroom TV, the hope at Channel 19 had always been to offer improved educational shows and charge participating school districts per student for the programming.

Doyle, who'd been granted a year's leave of absence from the newspaper, had an ambitious assignment. Her immediate task was to secure an adequate level of funding for ITV for the 1972-1973 school year by selling programming to the

From left, program director Torey Southwick, show host Walt Bodine, and general manager Zoel Parenteau discuss the changeover from KCSD to KCPT.

The Star's *Patricia Jansen Doyle and Robert Fuzy talk instructional TV.*

schools and charging a per capita fee. Also in her contract were suggested steps for long-term development of ITV.

A June 8 article in the *Raytown News* reported that the Raytown C-2 School Board had become the first to offer support to educational TV when it voted unanimously to pay $1.50 a student for the service. The district and its PTA would have to buy television sets for the schools, a need all of the ITV participants faced.

KCPT's monthly publication *Nineteen*, edited by volunteer Barbara Isaac, always included a program schedule and other items of interest to Channel 19 members. For example, a "Self Defense for Women" class, taught by a karate expert, began airing in April. It was reported that the instructor warned his pupils against practicing on husbands or boyfriends because "the male ego is a fragile thing."

'JOOOOLIA'

The June issue of Nineteen published a picture and some recipes of Julia Child, "The French Chef," a regular on Channel 19 with what *The Kansas City Star* called her "half-hour of kitchen cut-ups."

By that time, she was the toast of public TV and of Americans eager to learn how to prepare French cuisine. But 10 years earlier, her book, *The Art of French Cooking*, had just been published. Nobody outside of cooking schools had thought of watching chefs cook. The unknown author was invited to appear on a television program produced by WGBH, Boston's public TV station. Julia arrived armed with a hot plate, giant whisk and eggs and made an omelet.

With her weekly show "The French Chef," Julia Child became the toast of public television.

One of many Julia Child covers.

"Evening at the Pops" with Arthur Fiedler debuted on Channel 19 July 1972.

Carleton Scofield was interim general manager.

Viewers wanted to see more. WGBH produced three pilots, and then launched "The French Chef." Julia was widely acknowledged to be a driven perfectionist, but she was not afraid of making mistakes, and neither, she told her television audience, should they be.

On camera, she was inclined to say such things as "Hurray!" and "Yum yum." As she prepared a porker for *Cochon de Lait Roti,* she was urged to stop calling her entrée "him." In 1970, "The French Chef" went color, and commercial television tried to get her. But she preferred to stay with "the educators," as she called public TV.

The July issue of Nineteen pictured Arthur Fiedler, whose "Evening at the Pops," originating from Boston's Symphony Hall, appeared on Channel 19 that month for the first time.

At CSB, Zoel Parenteau's contract expired and a search committee led by attorney John Kreamer was appointed to identify a replacement. PBS aided the effort by supplying the names and credentials of several qualified candidates. In the meantime, Carleton Scofield was drafted as KCPT's interim general manager, a considerable career deviation for the learned University of Missouri-Kansas City chancellor emeritus. In a *Nineteen* column, Dr. Scofield expressed the CSB board's appreciation to Parenteau for his dedication to the establishment of public television in Kansas City.

Meanwhile, a small tempest erupted around the KCIT equipment that had

Meanwhile, a small tempest erupted around the KCIT equipment that had been purchased by CSB from RCA. Some of the equipment in the transmitter building wasn't included in the purchase agreement and was sold to a California company. In June, representatives of the purchaser appeared with trucks to claim their equipment but in the process began to remove items they had not purchased. CSB attorneys obtained a restraining order, preventing removal.

Workmen lowered Channel 50's antenna to the ground to make way for Channel 19's.

PRESIDENT VS. PRESS

On June 30, in a completely unexpected move, President Richard M. Nixon vetoed the two-year appropriation bill for public broadcasting that had been passed overwhelmingly by the House and the Senate. Reporting on government affairs was a pawn in the president's ongoing battle with the press, and the Nixon White House wanted it taken out of the hands of government-funded media. The Administration did not attack government affairs programming directly but focused on further decentralizing the public television system so that it would be less able to produce it.

The funding was restored. But the legacy of the quarrel was to perpetuate the public broadcasting system's reliance on local stations, rather than national centers, to produce programs — as it turned out, a blessing in disguise for KCPT.

The new Channel 19 antenna was installed at the top of the tower at 2100 Stark.

With local success came some potential pitfalls. As the community became aware of what a revitalized Channel 19 had to offer in the way of media exposure, noncommercial groups, some with an ax to grind, began to inquire about participation. In July, the program policy committee presented a policy statement to the CSB board to require that all programming be consistent with the purposes and objectives of CSB, and that there be balance and accountability in controversial programming.

The last visible sign of KCIT-TV in Kansas City was removed from KCPT's tower on July 15, when workmen lowered Channel 50's antenna to the ground, making room for Channel 19's new transmitting equipment. A powerful color signal was on the way.

In September, Unified School District No. 500 and the Kansas City School District both signed ITV contracts with CSB. By October, ITV was serving seven major school districts and several smaller public and parochial schools, reaching more than 170,000 children. CSB obtained TV sets for the participants from RCA at bargain prices.

New board president Joseph McDowell.

Dr. Charles Curran succeeded Carleton Scofield as interim GM.

In October, CSB adopted a complete employee pension plan. It had been developed by Mike Mayer, whose contributions to CSB ranged from serving as treasurer to auction major gifts chairman.

Also at its October meeting, the CSB Board again voted to increase its size, from 30 to 34. It added attorney John Kreamer, Butler Manufacturing Company vice president Roy Omundson, former Kansas City Mayor Ilus (Ike) W. Davis and Homer Wadsworth, who had previously declined board membership.

During his tenure as mayor, Davis would sometimes become exasperated with the many initiatives that came out of Wadsworth's Kansas City Association of Trusts and Foundations – and at one point proclaimed Wadsworth "the most dangerous man in Kansas City." In a *Kansas City Star* interview, the mayor complained that Wadsworth got things started, created a demand for them and then forced somebody else, "usually the city," to carry on. Now Davis was joining Wadsworth in something else he had started. But Davis would serve as a CSB director for many years, far outlasting Wadsworth in that role.

Demonstrating that KCPT would look to both sides of the state line for leadership, the board elected Joseph McDowell, the popular former mayor of Kansas City, Kan., my successor as president.

The executive committee discussed employing Dr. Charles Curran, second in command at the Kansas City Association of Trusts and Foundations, to succeed Dr. Scofield as interim general manager. Dr. Curran took the job, with the title of executive director. Although pressed into service in a totally unfamiliar role, the Harvard-educated Ph.D., with his background in philanthropy and city management, would perform admirably.

During his tenure, Curran's dedication to the success of the station was a major factor in its survival, as demonstrated by this anecdote from Jane Curran-Meuli:

> *I was a child when my father stepped into the leadership for Channel 19, so I do not know the details of his work within the operations of the station. Yet I clearly recall that he thought the price that the station was paying for taking care of the lawn was outrageous.*
>
> *So, on Saturday mornings, the two of us would load up the lawn mower in the trunk of the car and head over to the station, where he would mow and I was responsible for trimming.*

Viewers were fond of saying that Channel 19 produced "the best snow this side of the Rockies." The November issue of *Nineteen* quoted interim general manager Carleton Scofield announcing that that was no longer true:

(Continued on page 36)

Nixon Vetoes Public TV Bill

Washington (AP)—President Nixon unexpectedly vetoed a 2-year $155-million-dollar authorization bill for the Corporation for Public Broadcasting yesterday and called for passage of a 1-year, 46-million-dollar bill.

The move surprised congressional backers of the legislation but they said the ease with which the bill cleared Congress indicated chances are good for an override. The vetoed bill had passed the House, 256 to 69, and cleared the Senate, 82 to 1.

In his veto message to the House the President said the legislation "offers a poor approach to public broadcast financing. It ignores some serious questions which must be resolved before any long-range public broadcasting financing can be soundly devised, and before the statutory framework for public broadcasting is changed."

"Perhaps the most important one," Nixon said, "is the serious and widespread concern—expressed in Congress and within public broadcasting itself—that an organization, originally intended only to serve the local stations, is becoming instead the center of power and the focal point of control for the entire public broadcasting system."

Nixon said public broadcasting "can and does make important contributions to our nation's life by presenting educational and cultural programs of diversity and excellence" and it "deserves to be continued and to be strengthened."

He said, however, the bill does not place "adequate emphasis on localism" and "threatens to erode substantially public broadcasting's impressive potential for promoting innovative and diverse cultural and educational programing."

The bill's author, Rep. Torbert H. Macdonald (D-Mass.), chairman of the House communications subcommittee, said despite Nixon's "shallow protestations in yesterday's veto message, I am absolutely convinced that this administration has decided that their interests will best be served by muzzling the voice of public broadcasting directly."

Radio and television are too powerful in their eventual long-term effects for their control to intrusted to politicians — or businessmen.

— HUGH GREENE,
Director-General of the BBC, in 1959

(Continued from page 34)

> *October was a memorable month in the history of Channel 19. A picture, black and white, blurred, often buried in "snow," suddenly became clear, sharp, radiant in color.*

Volunteers and station staff helped raise $87,029.

Kansas City Chiefs star kicker Jan Stenerud was a celebrity auctioneer.

"It's a whole new ball game," Pat Doyle told *The Kansas City Star.*

KCPT expanded its coverage area by arrangements with 10 cable antenna systems, giving it increased power that would lead to even more distant CATV connections. Significant gifts from the Volker and Cowden foundations temporarily stabilized CSB's financial condition.

The TV tower would be another source of revenue from those wanting to lease space on it for antennas. There was an early lease with KBEY, later transferred to KBEQ (Wilks Broadcasting). Also leasing – Kansas City's public radio station, KCUR.

The March 20, 1973, meeting of the CSB executive committee was held in the Auction Warehouse (donated by Hallmark's Crown Center) as the station prepared for its first TV auction. Denny McWhinney, Mary Toevs and volunteer Karen Kraft led the execs on a warehouse tour.

That and the accompanying discussion underscored for the committee the enormity and complexity of the auction project as well as the organizational skills required of the co-sponsoring Kansas City Junior League and Chi Omega Sorority. The board extended a vote of thanks to the 215 volunteers who were making the auction both a reality and a success.

One of the auction items was a round of golf with pro golfer Tom Watson. Another was a 1973 Buick Special donated by Buick dealer Jerry Smith, an original CSB director and generous philanthropist, especially when children were involved. (The Jerry Smith Farm Park with its tall grass prairie remnant was donated to Kansas City by Smith and his wife.) Celebrity auctioneers included NFL Hall of Famers Len Dawson and Jan Stenerud.

In April, the board got the good news that the three-day auction had raised $87,029, more than expected. The resulting community interest and involvement were of even greater benefit to the station than the immediate relief in dollars and cents. The executive committee authorized Dr. Curran to create the staff position of auction coordinator for the 1974 auction and to offer the position to Denny McWhinney, volunteer chairman of the 1973 auction.

In a torrent of public broadcasting developments, program underwriting became permissible. The first series on Channel 19 underwritten by a local institution was "The Art of Animation," nine half-hour programs provided by the Mid-America Film Center of the Kansas City Art Institute and funded by a grant from the National Endowment for the Arts.

There would always be a fine line between the underwriting permitted by public television guidelines and commercial advertising. But underwriting made many of the programs enjoyed by Channel 19 viewers financially feasible. Some public television stations would come around to advocating open acceptance of commercial advertising, but KCPT management remained opposed.

In May, the search committee headed by John Kreamer proposed television professional Robert F. Fuzy of Chicago for the position of general manager. He took the position effective June 18, 1973.

Beginning in June, the Kansas City Art Institute presented 11 weekly half-hour programs for children, funded by grants from the Kansas City Municipal Art Commission and the National Endowment for the Arts.

By September, KCPT was on-air 16 hours a day, five days a week and eight hours on Sunday, with half of its programming devoted to schools.

An October report on the first year of Instructional TV experience described a very successful program that served nearly two-thirds of the school children in the metropolitan area. Included were instructional films produced elsewhere, stored in a central repository and "biked" by delivery van to schools upon demand. KCPT also was the first U.S. television station to carry programs from the Toronto Educational Communications Authority, a world leader in ITV. It had been a very good initial year for an ITV department of four people, huddled in an office that measured 10-by-7 feet.

Chicagoan Robert F. Fuzy became Channel 19's general manager in 1973.

Robert MacNeil and Jim Lehrer in the early days of the "Report."

MacNEIL AND LEHRER, BRITISH DRAMA AND 'WALL STREET WEEK'

The Watergate hearings in the fall of 1973 were covered nationally for PBS, gavel-to-gavel, by TV veteran Robert MacNeil, paired with rising star Jim Lehrer. They worked together harmoniously for four months. When the broadcast elicited an outpouring of favorable responses, the half-hour "MacNeil/Lehrer Report" became TV's first nightly news show.

Evening broadcasts brought British TV masterpieces. BBC programs such as "The Forsythe Saga" built an audience for American public television. One

(Continued on page 40)

DONATED BY

JERRY SMITH BUICK

A 1973 Century Luxus, 2-door Hard Top, Vinyl Roof, Midnight Blue.

Equipped with: Radio, heater, automatic transmission, White Wall Tires, Power Steering, Power Brakes, Air Conditioning.

STRONG SUPPORT for the Channel 19 Television Auction was evident from Jerry Smith as he presents the bill of sale for a 1973 Buick Century Luxus to Michael Mayer, chairman of the Major Gifts committee. The auction will be held April 6-7-8.

Top, Michael Mayer, right, major gifts chairman for the first auction, accepts the donation of a 1973 Buick Special from Buick dealer Jerry Smith. Above, quarterback Len Dawson was a noteworthy celebrity auctioneer.

Volunteers hustled to make Channel 19's first auction a success.

> Remember the good old time of black and white TV?
> It was mainly white.
> – WHOOPI GOLDBERG

Bank for "Wall Street Week," Columbia Union Bank for "Firing Line" and *The Kansas City Star* for the entire "Sesame Street" series. Also, that month KCPT produced "Meet the Candidates," a series of six programs introducing the candidates running for local office in the August primary.

In September, Ralph B. Rogers, chairman of the PBS Board of Governors, joined the CSB Board for dinner and some remarks. Rogers, a wealthy Dallas businessman, had assumed a major role in the reorganization of PBS that was being engineered by the public television stations. The result was to divorce PBS from the Corporation for Public Broadcasting and add a board of lay leaders.

In its new role, PBS introduced the Station Program Cooperative (SPC). It was a way for KCPT and other individual stations to select and pay for those nationally distributed programs that they wanted to broadcast, without the Corporation for Public Broadcasting playing a part in the decision-making process. Participation meant that Channel 19's viewers would be watching programs of their choice, but it also meant that the station would be paying thousands more than before to provide them. This led to more than the usual scrambling for dollars at KCPT.

Candidates appeared on Channel 19 before the August primary and the November general election.

CSB president Roy Omundson, left, and vice president John Kreamer, right, with PBS chairman Ralph Rogers, who had a major role in reorganizing PBS.

that the station had "moved from a period of newborn infancy fighting for financial survival up to adolescence, trying to do some new things."

KCPT continued to improve local political coverage. Candidates for elective office appeared on Channel 19 before the November 1974 elections: Senators Thomas Eagleton and Bob Dole; U.S. Reps. Larry Winn, William Randall and Jerry Litton; Martha Elizabeth Keys, who was running for Congress; and Robert F. Bennett, who was running for governor of Kansas. There also was a seminar series on the candidates for mayoral and city council elections.

On Nov. 17, Morton L. Sosland, nephew of KCPT founder Louis Sosland and editor of *Milling & Baking News*, appeared with "Firing Line's" Bill Buckley in a program taped at Crown Center and co-produced by Channel 19.

> *As my memory best recalls, I remember being terrified of doing this, and that was not helped by the day-before meeting with Buckley's producer-director, who put to me a series of "test questions" about American food aid. As I remember it, Buckley was not an advocate of American food aid, and I found myself defending it not just as a help to our foreign relations but also as a stimulus to the American agricultural economy at a time when exporting food products was in its post-World War II infancy.*
>
> *I knew that Buckley's success with this TV program was how he managed to put down guests who supposedly were experts in one field or another. This did not work with me, as I knew more about commodities and foreign food aid than he did, and, as a result, our program lacked the fireworks for which he was famous/infamous. I remember feeling good, very good, about how I did.*

Roy Omundsen, CSB president 1974-1976

"Firing Line's" William F. Buckley, Jr.

The evening of Dec. 9, 16 of Kansas City's top jazz groups jammed before Channel 19 cameras at the station, with guest performances by Les Milgram, chairman of Milgram Food Stores, and Mike White, newly elected Jackson County executive.

In December, Pat Doyle resigned as director of programming to accept a position at the Cleveland Foundation, and the CSB Board adopted a resolution of appreciation for her service.

It had been a very good three years.

1975 Home Box Office (HBO) appears, one of the new networks specifically designed for cable.

1977 The "Star Wars" movie is released and the TV miniseries "Roots" airs.

75

1977 ABC, traditionally a poor third behind NBC and CBS, becomes the nation's highest rated network. Some reasons: "Happy Days," "The Love Boat," "Charlie's Angels," "Family," "Taxi" and "Soap."

1979 Sony introduces the Walkman.

CHAPTER 3

DOCUMENTARIES AND MORE NATIONAL DRAMA

1975–1988

KCPT HAD A DEEP BENCH OF NATIONAL PROGRAMS. NOW IT WAS TIME TO ADD MORE LOCAL AFFAIRS SHOWS AND JOIN THE CLUB OF PBS STATIONS PRODUCING THEIR OWN DOCUMENTARIES. THERE WAS NO LETUP IN THE NATIONAL DEBATE OVER WHO SHOULD PAY FOR PUBLIC TV AND HOW MUCH CONTROL THE FUNDERS SHOULD HAVE. IN 1980, A NATIONAL PBS OFFERING, "DEATH OF A PRINCESS," SEVERELY TESTED THE FOURTH NETWORK'S ABILITY TO RESIST CENSORSHIP. KCPT AIRED THE PROGRAM — WHICH DRAMATIZED THE TRUE STORY OF THE EXECUTION OF A SAUDI PRINCESS FOR ADULTERY — BUT MANY STATIONS DID NOT.

1980 Ted Turner, who would later in life say he preferred a good book or a good conversation to television, establishes Cable News Network (CNN).

1981 President Ronald Reagan, a former television show host, begins to show great skill in exploiting the media.

1983 The finale of the TV series M*A*S*H* is the most-watched episode in U.S. history.

1986 The Space Shuttle Challenger 10 explodes 73 seconds after liftoff.

1987 On "Black Monday," Oct. 19, the Dow plunges 508 points, the largest drop in Wall Street history.

88

"Firing Line" with William F. Buckley.

The cast of "Monty Python's Flying Circus."

Setting up for "Meet the Candidates."

A "Meet the Candidates" episode.

1974 HAD ENDED on a high note.

Channel 19 had been on the air (as KCPT) only four years. But in that time, it had become the only place on the dial for such popular national shows as "Sesame Street," "The MacNeil/Lehrer Report," "NOVA," "Firing Line," "Upstairs/Downstairs," "Evening at the Pops" and "The French Chef." The station was broadcasting 16 hours a day, five days a week, and eight hours on Sundays.

In June 1975, it began all-day Saturday programming, a move that permitted KCPT to add "Monty Python's Flying Circus" to its entertainment lineup. The BBC import was puzzling to some, addictive to many and just another example of the innovative programming public TV could provide. Highly intellectual, zany, often political, it lampooned the idiosyncrasies of the British professional class. The half-hour program featured illustration, as well as sketch comedy that was often surreal, risqué and hard to describe – thus the coining of the term *Pythonesque.*

Channel 19 was now on the air seven nights a week; Sunday morning was the only hole in the schedule. The Community Service Broadcasting (CSB) board enlarged to 36, and the 1975 auction raised more than $115,000. Those charged with looking ahead began to see that the station's physical facilities were becoming more and more inadequate.

Locally produced shows, meanwhile, had just gotten out of the gate, led by such programs as "Your Congressman," "Kansas City Looks at Washington," "Meet the Candidates" and "The Art of Animation." The way forward was clear: Develop quality local programming.

The small staff found the resources to hire a former newspaper reporter as a producer and began to add more local and regional programs to the schedule.

The January 1975 *19 Guide* announced that KCPT had been awarded the largest grant ever to aid in producing a local program: "Oren Lee Staley and the NFO." The money came from the Central Education Network (CEN), an association of 35 stations in 12 Midwestern states. Staley was a charismatic farm leader from St. Joseph, Mo. As president of the National Farmer's Organization (NFO), he preached more power to farmers, especially economic independence in setting their own prices for crops and livestock. He was well known in agriculture circles, and he was eloquent.

Willis Rowell, the group's historian, in his book *Mad as Hell,* recounts the time when the NFO ran out of money and the Securities and Exchange Commission

Television is more interesting than people.
If it were not, we should have people standing in the corners of our rooms.

– ALAN COREN,
British humor writer

sued to force it into receivership. At the brink of the court hearing, Rowell wrote, Staley called a meeting in Des Moines and thousands of farmers attended. When he finished speaking, a Brinks truck was called in to receive the results – contributions of $5.2 million in cash, checks and canceled loan obligations.

"Oren Lee Staley and the NFO" resonated with Midwestern viewers. It was narrated and produced by a former WDAF hire, John Masterman.

KCPT got a grant to make "Oren Lee Staley and the N.F.O.," produced by new hire John Masterman.

LONG-FORM DOCUMENTARIES

On Aug. 12, 1975, "Not Forgotten: Harry Truman" was broadcast by Channel 19. It was produced at the Truman Library in Independence under another grant from CEN and featured interviews with Margaret Truman Daniel and James Whitmore, star of the stage production "Give 'em Hell, Harry." Masterman was co-producer of the telecast.

A former newspaper reporter, Masterman had begun at Channel 19 as a program producer/host and then was added as a full-time employee with the title of director of public affairs – a real coup for the station.

He had a Pulitzer Prize. In 1961 with the Amarillo, Texas, *Globe Times*, Masterson was the principal reporter on a series of stories that won the Pulitzer for meritorious public service. He'd been a reporter for NBC, an anchor for WNBC-TV New York and an NBC news correspondent in Israel, Libya, England and Ireland. His peers at the network were such TV giants as John Chancellor and the Huntley-Brinkley team.

Masterman co-produced "Not Forgotten: Harry Truman."

He began his 19-year association with KCPT at an opportune time. Public television was already getting a name for its long-form documentaries. One of his major projects was a documentary film on the Missouri River, financed by a $62,000 grant from the Environmental Protection Agency.

On the public affairs side, his signature program, "Kansas City Illustrated," aired weekly and employed six reporters. He also produced and hosted the series "The Kansas City Round Table," where among others he interviewed L.P. Cookingham, Kansas City's dean of city managers, as well as candidates for election to the Kansas City School Board.

Masterman also hosted "Kansas City Roundtable."

It was ironic, as well as painful, that the Kansas City School District, innovative originator of Channel 19's instructional television service, was compelled for

(Continued on page 49)

Top, John Masterman on the set of "Kansas City Illustrated"; above, with his KC Illustrated crew in 1983.

(Continued from page 47)
financial reasons to withdraw from ITV. The loss of that contract required budget cuts in local television productions amounting to $57,850.

But at the Oct. 14, 1975, annual meeting, station manager Bob Fuzy reported significant increases in both ITV and public broadcast hours and a revenue increase of 24 percent, thanks in part to improvement in membership and underwriting income.

John Kreamer was elected CSB president, Laura Kemper of Commerce BancShares Inc. was named a vice president, and Hallmark executive Robert Stark was the new secretary.

On April 15, 1976, the board voted to change the corporate name. The Channel 19 licensee would now be "Public Television 19, Inc." (PT 19).

At its June 9 meeting, the board noted with deep regret the untimely death of founding director and generous supporter Louis Sosland and welcomed Mrs. Rheta Sosland as his replacement.

Even with revenue increases, quality instructional television was in jeopardy at Channel 19 without participation by the Kansas City School District. The board decided to carry on for the 1976-'77 school year but then re-examine the future of ITV.

The Republican Party in September 1976 held its national convention in Kansas City. The convention was covered by four national PBS programs, including "Washington Week in Review." "The MacNeil/Lehrer Report's" national broadcast of the convention emanated from KCPT's studios. A September 13 letter from "MacNeil/Lehrer's" executive producer thanked Robert Fuzy and his staff:

> *Despite our demands, all of you responded with hard work and good humor and the result was a week of programs of which to be proud.*

On occasion, KCPT pre-empted scheduled PBS programs with special telecasts. This happened in September, when "NOVA" was ousted in favor of a Canada Cup hockey game. Not every viewer was pleased with the exchange.

Also in September, KCPT introduced "Kansas City Strip," a weekday series of half-hour programs at 6:30 p.m., each with its own theme: "The Scene" (arts and entertainment), "Roundtable" (interviews with community leaders), "The Arena" (a call-in show with studio audience participation), "Human Beings" (showcasing notables) and "Marketplace" (local economy and business).

Laura Kemper of Commerce BancShares became board vice president in 1975.

Hallmark executive Robert Stark was named secretary.

"Kansas City Strip" with moderator Steve Dawson, formerly of KCTV5.

Above, "KC Strip" with, from left, producer Dave Welsh, guest Steve Allen, moderator John Jessup. Top, on the set with Allen and Jessup.

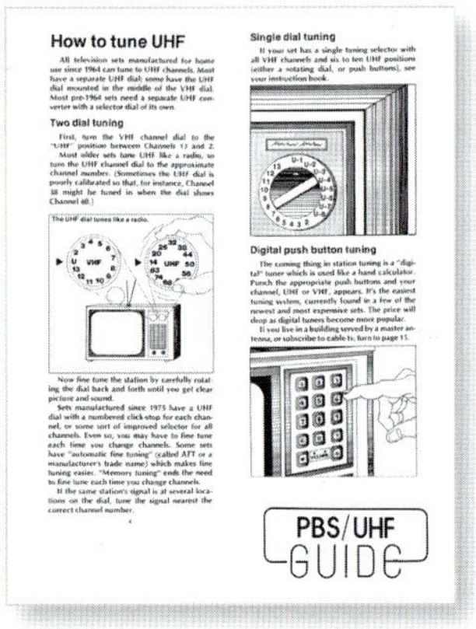

Some viewers needed a tip sheet.

PBS president Larry Grossman, left, and KCPT president Robert Fuzy at a Channel 19 preview party.

The show came on after the local commercial television newscasts and consolidated KCPT's public affairs and community programming into a single time slot. *The Kansas City Times* heralded the new program in a column by television editor Joyce Wagner:

> *In a long-awaited and much overdue move, KCPT television, Channel 19, finally will begin offering viewers this season local programming on a regular basis through an innovative series entitled Kansas City Strip.*

On the national scene, PBS installed a satellite interconnection system and began charging each participating public television station part of the $138,000 cost of its satellite receiving terminal. Channel 19, whose terminal site was at 2100 Stark Ave., would have to contribute $15,000 and PBS would pay the balance. PBS would then distribute programming via satellite instead of by AT&T lines and microwave. The system was feeding four separate programs at a time, one aired immediately and the other three taped for later broadcast.

On Oct. 2, 1976, a *Kansas City Times* editorial heralded Channel 19's 15th year of broadcasting. After noting that "its UHF assignment on the TV dial leaves it vulnerable to viewer oversight," the article concluded:

> *Channel 19 is worth the effort to locate it on the dial and certainly is worth the contributions it needs so greatly.*
> *(A PBS/UHF Guide provided instructions for "How to Tune UHF.")*

In November, PBS president Larry Grossman attended a Channel 19 preview party to honor the nationwide broadcast and public TV premier of the "Bicentennial Hall of Fame Dramas," a trilogy on presidents Washington, Lincoln and Truman termed the "television Mount Rushmore."

The three programs were a gift to public television from Kansas City's Hallmark Cards, donated after the programs first aired on NBC. The first of the series, "Valley Forge," aired Nov. 9 and starred Richard Basehart as George Washington. It was followed by "The Rivalry" (Abraham Lincoln) on Nov. 16, and "Truman at Potsdam" on Nov. 23. In announcing the gift, Donald J. Hall, president of Hallmark, said: "All of us associated with the Hallmark Hall of Fame are pleased to have this opportunity to demonstrate our support of public television."

(Continued on page 53)

In 1976, KCPT installed a new satellite receiving terminal at the Stark Street location, shortly before the staff moved to 125 E. 31st St.

Above, the KCMO-TV building when Channel 19 bought it. Top, a vintage photo of KCMO.

(Continued from page 50)

GETTING 600 PERCENT BIGGER

Then, a Nov. 11 press release announced a major acquisition: KCPT had agreed with the Meredith Corporation to purchase the KCMO-TV building and parking lot at 125 E. 31st St. in Kansas City. KCMO's bargain price of $220,000 was only half the appraised value. The move from Stark to East 31st would increase operating space by 600 percent and allow the TV auction to be housed in the station's own facility. (KCMO was moving to Fairway, Kan.)

To pay for the property, KCPT would launch its first capital fund drive, with Faultless Starch/Bon Ami Co. CEO Gordon Beaham III, a member of the KCPT board, as chairman. The goal was $675,000, the amount of the purchase price for the KCMO building plus miscellaneous items, including the cost of some new cameras. The Enid and Crosby Kemper Foundation and the Hallmark Educational Fund were large initial contributors. Other significant donors: the Parker B. Francis III Foundation, George E. Powell and the Powell Family Foundation.

Back in 1974, KCPT had joined the Station Program Cooperative (SPC) as a way to exercise choice over which nationally distributed programs it wanted to pay for and broadcast. The investment paid off in February 1977, when members of Channel 19 voted their entertainment preferences on a Viewer's Choice Ballot and the station purchased 16 popular programs through PBS.

Display of items up for auction.

Auctioneer Mary Loy Brown on live mike.

Volunteers take bids over the phone.

From left, George E. Powell Jr., Nicholas K. Powell, Marjorie Powell Allen, George E. Powell III and Marilyn Powell of The Powell Family Foundation.

KCPT auctions became affairs where the whole community pitched in to help, including other local TV stations that normally would have been competitors.

Laurel Defoe came to KCPT from WDAF-TV.

A documentary film on the Missouri River was financed by the Environmental Protection Agency.

The April TV auction, now a six-day community effort by more than 1,200 volunteers, brought in more than $162,000. A telethon on the night of the final episode of "Upstairs/Downstairs" generated $12,161 more, with 550 individual pledges. One of the auction sale items was the 600-square-foot office trailer at 21st and Stark, a vestige of the KCIT-TV bankruptcy sale.

On May 17, 1977, KCPT broadcast John Masterman's "The Mighty Missouri." It was PT 19's first major documentary effort, filmed at more than 150 locations in nine states. The film was written, produced and directed by Masterman and Laurel Defoe, a former WDAF-TV reporter who had joined KCPT in 1976 as assistant public affairs producer. It was made available to PBS stations and regional networks and was distributed in a 12-state area.

In July 1977, Robert Fuzy's title was changed to executive vice president and general manager. He was now a corporate officer of Public Television 19 Inc.

On Sept. 8, 1977, Yellow Freight Systems' vice-president George Powell III was elected to fill a vacancy on the PT board. The Powell family had continued the generosity of George III's grandfather, one of the station's founders, and the board greeted the new director with enthusiasm.

At the annual meeting, Robert Stark replaced John Kreamer as president and Steven Smith became the new secretary. Channel 19 now had 100,000 Kansas City-area children enrolled in ITV, with 3.2 video lessons a week per child, the country's best utilization rate. Forty percent of the enrolled ITV schools were on the Kansas side.

By 1978, there were 280 stations reaching 80 percent of American households, and nearly two-thirds of them were tuning in to public TV at least once a month.

CARNEGIE II AND THE BEDLAM THAT BROUGHT IT

It had been a little over a decade since the Public Broadcasting Act was passed. Public TV stations, funded in part by federal appropriations, were now broadcasting under the protection of the First Amendment. The Nixon administration's attempt to dictate program content had been turned back, and the stations had independence. They received most of their support locally. The Corporation for Pubic Broadcasting (CPB), while acting as a vehicle for federal funding, was also expected to shield them from political influence.

The attitude toward public TV under the Ford and Carter administrations ranged from benignly indifferent to supportive. However, in July 1978, bills before Congress to extend appropriations for public broadcasting threatened to convert CPB into a quasi-governmental agency, meaning an arm of the government would be overseeing program decision-making.

The 19 Guide heralded the station's fifth TV 19 auction.

At the press conference announcing sale of the KCMO building to KCPT: from left, KCPT capital fund drive chairman Gordon T. Beaham III, KCMO's general manager Charles H. McAbee, KCPT president John H. Kreamer and general manager Robert F. Fuzzy.

It seemed as though someone was always debating the value of public TV.

Reflecting the struggles around creative independence, minority representation and funding for public television, in 1977 the Carnegie Commission had established a second commission on The Future of Public Broadcasting (termed Carnegie II). According to the authoritative *Public Radio and Television in America: A Political History,* by Ralph Engelman, the Carnegie Commission attributed the creation of the new commission to "the failure of public broadcasting to fulfill the mission enunciated in 1967." Joan Ganz Cooney, president of Children's Television Workshop, was widely quoted as suggesting that "Sesame Street" could not have been launched in the current chaotic state of public broadcasting.

The 1979 Carnegie II report, "A Public Trust," endorsed higher levels of funding and proposed sweeping structural changes, including the elimination of CPB, but attracted little public attention.

CPB survived these assaults, but new federal legislation was passed that required each station affiliate to establish a diversified Community Advisory Board by April 30, 1979. The law recommended a seven-member board.

Although the CSB board was already varied, members amended the bylaws to provide for such a body, to even further reflect the diverse interests and needs of the communities served by KCPT. Its role as overseer was to be advisory only.

A $100,000 grant from the State of Kansas funded the purchase of a videotape recorder and accessories for the station. And $36,000 from the National Endowment for the Humanities funded development of a script for a 90-minute program on the lore of the Great Plains.

KCPT staff completed the move to 31st Street in March 1978. One acre of the Stark Street property was sold; PT 19 retained the other nine acres, including the KCPT broadcast tower. (Today, there is a large Verizon Wireless building on that property, for which Verizon remits a significant monthly payment to KCPT.) The April 1978 Program Guide noted that $504,191 had been raised in the capital fund drive to help pay for the relocation. The week of April 17 saw the first auction held at the KCPT station.

The KCMO-TV tower remains in place today, a prominent part of the midtown skyline, and continues to serve KCMO and its viewers. After winter storms, ice sometimes falls from the tower, piercing the KCPT station roof, and on occasion KCPT staffers wear hard hats for protection when venturing outside. The tower is also a very large lightning rod, attracting spectacular and sometimes electronically damaging lightning strikes.

(Continued on page 58)

KCPT headquarters with the familiar, looming KCMO tower.

Producer John Jessup, left, and director Steve Baker at the production control switcher.

Jo Ellen (Hull) Brisbane generates characters for titles at the Chyron keyboard.

At an A/V recorder in the master control room.

Master control room in the KCPT building.

(Continued from page 56)

After much effort by the station staff, KCPT was named the public station on the Columbia, Mo., cable system.

The ITV program continued to grow. An update at the October 1978 annual meeting reported that 11 school districts had been added and a six-school pilot project in the Kansas City district appeared promising. The availability of functioning TV equipment was the most serious obstacle to attracting new districts, and Kansas City schools were applying for a federal grant for this purpose. The board heard a proposal for federal funding to pay for reintroduction of ITV into the district's elementary schools and several junior high schools. It learned that the greatest amount of Channel 19 broadcast airtime was allocated for PBS programs, but ITV was the second largest component.

A microwave signal link between the studio at 125 E. 31st St. and the transmitter at 2100 Stark failed in frigid January 1979. KCMO-TV came to the rescue, making available its portable microwave equipment. "It was a life-saving gesture," said Bob Fuzy.

At the April 15, 1979, board meeting, members were appointed to the Community Advisory Board mandated by new federal legislation. Attorney Lee Vertis Swinton resigned from the PT 19 board in order to be named chairman of the community board.

An August 1979 "Fact Sheet" recited the history and current status of KCPT/Channel 19:

> *Transmitter, tower and earth station receiver remained at 2100 Stark but everything else was now at 125 East 31st Street— offices, studios and renovated master control area. A staff of 40 full-time employees included John Masterman's documentary film unit and new arrival Michael Murphy, an intern destined to become a talented fixture at the station.* (Murphy had been pressed into service as a pinch hitter, a cameraman for a pledge drive — the beginning of a love affair with KCPT that endures to this day.)
>
> *Eighty percent of KCPT's operating funds came from the community. 1,100 hours of ITV broadcasts were comprised of programs or lessons for kindergarten through 12th grade and in-service teacher training. Non-instructional programming consisted of nearly 4,000 hours. Series programs included "Kansas City Strip," and there were KCPT-produced documentaries. Children's programs featured "Sesame Street" and "The Electric Company," still the gold standard for children's programs.*
>
> *Theater and movies included many BBC-produced classics such as*

"The Six Wives of Henry VIII" and "I Claudius." For music, there were "Evening at the Pops" and other performances still familiar today, and public affairs broadcasts ranged from regularly scheduled weekly programs (e.g., "The MacNeil/Lehrer Report") to prime time coverage of major events of national importance. Also, series of general interest: "Wall Street Week" and "Nova," for example.

Channel 19 had come a long way since bankruptcy auction days.

Sister Olive Louise Dallavis, president of Avila College.

UMKC Chancellor Dr. George Russell became a board member.

At the October 1979 annual meeting, members learned that Kansas City ITV program pilot schools had expanded to 17, and there would be another 18 the following year. Charles Battey, executive vice president of United Telecommunications, succeeded Robert Stark as PT 19 president. Board members now included James H. Hale, president and publisher of *The Kansas City Star* and *Times;* Sister Olive Louise Dallavis, president of Avila College; and Dr. George A. Russell, chancellor of the University of Missouri-Kansas City.

Peter Duchin's Orchestra entertained at an October benefit tea dance at the remodeled Harzfeld's Plaza store. Hosted by Harzfeld's and co-chaired by Mrs. Sally Kemper Wood, Mrs. Eugene Brown and patron of the arts David Stickelber, it raised $6,300 for Channel 19.

In November 1979, "The 12th Street Rag," a 60-minute program on the evolution of ragtime music in the Missouri Valley, aired on Channel 19. It featured the Kansas City Philharmonic Orchestra, and most of it was taped in Kansas City with special assistance from KCPT.

Mike Murphy (foreground) and Randy Mason both give directions to cameramen inside the KCPT studio while producing the arts and entertainment program at the KCPT station.

A docudrama that literally became an international incident.

The KCPT Channel 19 Instructional TV training manual.

Charles Battey, KCPT's last lay president.

PBS KICKS THE HORNET'S NEST, KCPT STEPS UP

On May 12, 1980, PBS stirred up a hornet's nest with its broadcast of "Death of a Princess" — a program many stations opted not to show. It was a true story. The princess was a young member of the Saudi royal family, publicly executed with her lover for committing adultery. The story was conveyed by dramatizing dozens of interviews with Saudis who said they had either watched or were familiar with the execution. It was co-produced by England's Associated Television Corporation and the WGBH Educational Foundation (affiliated with Boston public television station WGBH).

First shown in Britain, the docudrama angered the Saudis, whose protest reportedly included threats to impose sanctions on British business interests and break formal ties with the United Kingdom. The U.S. government was pressured to censor the broadcast. Mobil Oil, which had extensive interests in Saudi Arabia *and* was a major PBS funder, placed critical ads in newspapers. Members of Congress, worried about oil supplies, spoke out against airing the program. PBS viewers reportedly were calling and writing 4-to-1 against showing the film. One could say it was a do-or-die moment for the broadcast independence PBS stations had sought. And one cannot help but wonder what would happen today.

PBS withstood the efforts at suppression. "We plan to schedule the program," PBS president Larry Grossman said in response to the pressures. "It's a program of integrity, it was made responsibly, and we intend to broadcast it."

KCPT broadcast the film, a highly controversial decision. Thirty-eight PBS stations in 13 states did not, and 46 stations delayed its broadcast. Board members discussed the furor surrounding the airing of the film at a June 1980 meeting. While the vast majority of calls before the broadcast were unfavorable, there was general approval of the showing afterward.

Meanwhile on the instructional TV front, KCPT projected that the Shawnee Mission district would participate in an ITV pilot program in the 1980-'81 school year. Other Kansas programs: development of a process to provide ITV to south-east Kansas schools, and 1,800 hours of ITV to the Coffeyville and Fredonia school districts. The Kansas City district was continuing to increase its ITV commitment.

A position paper submitted to the PT 19 executive committee in 1980 had noted that, of material broadcast by the station to general audiences, 97.5 percent originated somewhere else – despite the interest in local affairs, Channel 19 was not primarily a producer. It was too expensive.

However, there were exceptions. On Nov. 15, 1980, KCPT aired "The Urban Future" examining the changes that city governments would undergo in years ahead, and featuring Kansas City's city manager Robert Kipp. On Nov. 26, PBS broadcast "The Harvest Run," a one-hour KCPT documentary about the custom crews that harvested 40 percent of the U.S. wheat crop, the country's most important agricultural export. Both programs were produced by Masterman and Defoe.

A March 1981 pledge drive generated $185,000, with calls from 4,400 families. And successful TV Auctions continued – the 1981 auction produced a record $213,000.

In April, the documentary "Ozark Storytelling" premiered, presented by KCPT. It was produced by local filmmaker John Altman. PBS later distributed the program nationally. The picturesque mountain region had fascinating stories to tell, as colorful Ozark raconteurs demonstrated.

The first telecast of the July Fourth Concert on the Capitol Mall in Washington, D.C., was aired by PBS and enjoyed by KCPT viewers. It is now an annual national observance.

Masterman and Defoe often collaborated on documentaries.

TRAGEDY AT THE HYATT

In July 1980, the Kansas City Hyatt Regency Hotel's second- and fourth-floor walkways collapsed at a dance in the atrium lobby. It was a monumental structural failure in a building only one year old; 114 people were killed and another 200 injured. The disaster was covered by "The McNeil/Lehrer Report," originating through Channel 19.

Chairman Gad Smith

At the Oct. 15, 1981, annual meeting, the PT 19 bylaws were amended to create the office of chairman and to change the title of the station manager to president. Charles Battey completed a two-year term as KCPT's last lay president, and his successor, attorney Gad Smith, was elected chairman. The station's financial condition was precarious when Battey took office. (Fuzy told him it was "teetering.") Now the organization's financial condition was good enough that the departing Battey cautioned the board "not to become euphoric because of the station's present healthy and sound condition."

KCPT 19 director William G. Skelly

When the state of Missouri created a Public Telecommunication Authority, PT 19 director William G. Skelly, a Kansas City Southern Industries executive, was one of three Missouri General Assembly appointees to the governing board. The authority would oversee construction of "translator" towers in remote areas of the state, making public TV broadcasts available to residents there.

"Kansas City Illustrated" premiered in 1982, replacing "Kansas City Strip." KCPT's primary local production series, it was a one-hour telecast covering the Kansas City region hosted by John Masterman. Randy Mason, director of production and local programming for Sunflower Cablevision in Lawrence, Kan., admired the program and contacted Masterman expressing an interest in employment at KCPT. Mason was hired as one of four reporters for "Kansas City Illustrated's" second year. Like Mike Murphy, he was there to stay, despite other opportunities.

(Continued on page 64)

THE KANSAS CITY STAR

TV Radio & Pop Music scene

Program Guid
Oct. 31-Nov. 6

Jane Fonda

... will appear in a sketch
On The Great American Dream Machine

Two Kansas City Star TV *magazine covers indelibly brand the era.*

KCPT staff built the station's first remote truck from Army surplus vehicles. The box-like unit above sat on the truck bed, right, when it was driven to cover such events as Kansas City Chief's camp in Liberty. Relic of a can-do era, it now rests in a field in Greenwood, Mo.

© JOHN LONG

British export "Dr. Who" had a Kansas City fan base.

Comedian Mark Russell gave several benefit performances.

(Continued from page 67)

a mobile BBC exhibit in a 48-foot-long trailer featuring the series' monsters and villains with sound effects and animation, visited KCPT studios.

In December, the board learned of a three-year grant from the Parker B. Francis Foundation to be applied to the match for the NTIA equipment grant. John Francis had served as a CSB vice president, and the Francis family had been financially supportive; this was their largest gift to date to KCPT. There also was a grant from the Courtney S. Turner Trust, another faithful supporter.

In 1987, Wichita had discontinued its ITV program and joined KCPT's program. Bob Fuzy announced that the result was an added $34,000 in ITV annual income. Channel 19 now served more than 300,000 students in Missouri and Kansas. The station ranked fourth in viewership among the eleven largest UHF markets.

TV AUCTIONS ENTER THE BIG TIME

Aided by donations of a 1988 Nissan automobile and a 1960 BMW, and simulcasts by all four commercial TV stations, the April 1988 TV auction produced a record $358,322.

Floyd May, CAB chairman, had previously stated that the CAB board was considering changing from a discussion group to an "action" group. Later, at his request, the CAB Board was enlarged from 15 to 20 members. In June, May reported to the PT 19 board that the CAB board did not feel that KCPT producers were meeting the needs of various minority groups and would like station management to address this issue.

The PT 19 board accepted the report and asked Bob Fuzy to examine the CAB concerns and return with his findings. Later, the executive committee approved the station management's conduct with respect to minority programming. The CAB would subsequently become perhaps the most active advisory board in public television – in representing the diverse KCPT viewing area and its activities in support of KCPT.

George Powell III, now the president of Yellow Freight Systems, was elected chairman of Public Television 19 at the October 1988 annual meeting. Jacquie Mayer, who had chaired a September Mark Russell benefit performance, announced that the humorous, nonpartisan political satirist and PBS regular had produced a profit for KCPT of $30,000.

The December Holiday Special featured the Kansas City Symphony and the King's Singers of England, a male a capella sextet, taped during a live performance before a full house at Kansas City's Lyric Theatre. It was shown by PBS on 30 public television stations across the country.

David Welsh, KCPT director of broadcasting, explained the motivation:

> *So why did we do the program? It was not only a good idea, it gave the Kansas City Symphony its second national TV production, and KCPT gave a Kansas City Christmas music performance (with a bit of an English accent) to the rest of the country.*
>
> (The Symphony production became a PBS Christmas staple and also was available on video cassette.)

As it turned out, the circumvention of Yuletide fundraisers had been only a temporary reprieve. This year, there was a reversion to the December pledge drive, in which Peter, Paul and Mary and local radio stars made special guest appearances.

George Powell III was elected chairman in 1988.

KCPT broadcasting director Dave Welsh.

The Francis Family Foundation, in 2001 photo, was a major KCPT funder. Seated from left: Peggy Dunn, John B. Francis, Mary Harris Francis and Susan Francis Neves. Standing from left: Ramon Murgia, Robert West, Spence Heddons, Scott Francis, Ann Francis Burhum, David V. Francis, Robert Reintjes, James Sunderland and Charles Curran.

Ken Burns and Buck O'Neil visit the final resting place of "the greatest pitcher of them all."

89

1989 Home videocassette recorders are widely available, allowing viewers to record and replay programs on their own time.

1989 The animated satiric adventures of a working class family in the city of Springfield first airs. It's called "The Simpsons."

1990 The PBS documentary "The Civil War" attracts one of the largest audiences ever for public broadcasting.

1990 It will be the decade of the news-magazine. To "60 Minutes" and ABC's "20/20" is added "Dateline NBC" and CBS's "Eye to Eye with Connie Chung."

1991 Pictures of U.S. bombs falling on Baghdad in the Persion Gulf War show TV's handmaiden role when history is being made.

CHAPTER 4

THE POLITICS OF PROGRAMMING

1989–1994

William F. Buckley, Jim Lehrer and Ken Burns all visited Kansas City on KCPT business. Burns came to town to mark the debut of his documentary series "Baseball," which beat out his "The Civil War" as the most watched program in PBS history. Controversial programs aired by Channel 19 included an exclusive interview with Kansas City serial killer Robert Berdella and news magazines and dramas presenting nonjudgmental views of gay and lesbian life. Meanwhile, KCPT was deepening its roots in the community and had the largest instructional TV program in the country. More than 80 percent of U.S. households tuned in to public TV at least once a month.

1992 Viewers feast on "X-Men," a small-screen retelling of the comic book series in which a team of mutant superheroes fights for justice and human acceptance.

1993 With the Internet becoming a fact of life, TV news organizations develop email systems and websites to communicate with the public in a new way.

1994 Many stations carry almost every minute of the trial of former football star O.J. Simpson for the murder of his wife, and spend evening hours dissecting the day's courtroom events.

1994 Former Arkansas state employee Paula Jones files a federal lawsuit against President Clinton for sexual harassment.

94

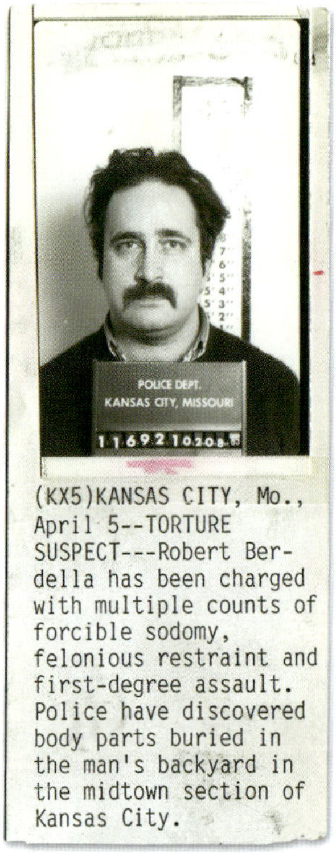

Robert Berdella's police booking mug shot.

CHANNEL 19 banked a record $358,322 from the April 1988 TV auction, but the perennial search for dollars to run the station, pay salaries and buy programming continued. After fits and starts, studies and surveys, KCPT initiated a capital fund drive. The goal: $5 million over five years. A Francis Family Foundation contribution was a good start.

In January 1989, KCPT aired an exclusive interview with Robert Berdella, a serial killer who drugged and tortured young men at his home in Kansas City's sedate Hyde Park neighborhood. He was apprehended after his sixth known victim jumped from the second story of the house and ran naked and bloody down the street wearing only a dog collar. The narrative that unfolded was gruesome but almost impossible to turn away from. Police found several hundred polaroid photographs and a detailed torture log. He had met several of his victims at his business, a small shop called Bob's Bizarre Bazaar. After torturing them for days or weeks, Berdella would drain their blood, cut up the bodies and put them out in the trash for Monday morning pickup.

Kansas City police dig for evidence in Berdella's backyard, April 7, 1988.

> Television is just another appliance. It's a toaster with pictures. Let the people decide through the marketplace mechanisms what they wish to see and hear. Why is there this national obsession to tamper with this box of transistors and tunes when we don't do the same for *Time* magazine?
>
> – MARK FOWLER,
> chairman, U.S. Federal Communications Commission

The announcement of the Channel 19 interview with Berdella generated a flood of angry telephone calls before the telecast, but there was also much viewer curiosity and most comments afterward were favorable. KCPT was first in ratings for that particular prime time hour, the highest in station history, and its audience for the entire month increased by 10 percent over the previous January.

The January 28 preshow party for a touring production of "Sesame Street Live" attracted 350 people to Kansas City's Municipal Auditorium, where a performance followed the party. Big Bird was now 40 years old, and some of his earliest friends were parents in the audience.

At the April PT 19 board meeting, the directors watched a video of community leaders explaining why they favored a minority program that had been proposed by KCPT's Community Advisory Board (CAB). Meanwhile, the durable "Hoy in Kansas City" remained on the air. Originally produced by Rudy Padilla on a volunteer basis, it now was produced by KCPT with KMBC-TV's Maria Antonia hosting. (It was succeeded in 1993 by "Viva Kansas City.")

By June, KCPT had the country's largest Instructional TV (ITV) program, serving more than 350,000 students in 343 school districts. Forty-one media specialists worked with school librarians to select an extensive video library supporting Missouri and Kansas learning objectives. Programs were then broadcast according to a published schedule. Eight centers provided videotapes for about 75,000 students outside the Channel 19 signal reach. There were 47,400 students in the Wichita area. A KCPT staff member was based there as the station's Regional Educational Services representative.

To help distinguish Channel 19's regional focus from competing national satellite and cable school television programs, KCPT produced a Missouri and Kansas history series, "History Weavers," which gave kindergarten to sixth-grade students a glimpse of area history through the eyes of accomplished Missouri and Kansas storytellers. More than 300 teacher training workshops provided instruction to member schools, colleges and parent and professional educator groups on how to integrate ITV programs into their lessons.

The PBS American Masters series featured Kansas City's jazz genius Charlie "Bird" Parker in July. It was while hanging around Kansas City clubs, listening to the masters who passed through town, that Parker gained his real jazz education. Part of the program told the story of another fabled Kansas City musician, Jay McShann.

Jazz saxophonist and Beat Generation icon Charlie Parker was featured on PBS' American Masters series.

William F. Buckley taped two "Firing Line" episodes at KCPT.

"The Lawrence Welk" show ran almost 28 years on ABC before going into syndication.

In September, a board governance committee chaired by William Skelly recommended some changes. The board's size was cumbersome, and director participation was becoming difficult to schedule. The board adopted the proposal that the full board would meet quarterly and interim committee activity would be emphasized between meetings.

That same month Bruce Christenson, president and CEO of PBS, was a guest speaker at the KCPT Underwriters' Luncheon at the Kansas City Club. According to *A History of Public Broadcasting*, Christenson was an effective diplomat, credited with "helping the system withstand both internal and external attacks" during his nine-year tenure at PBS.

LUNCH WITH BILL BUCKLEY

The entire board had lunch at the Kansas City Club in October with "Firing Line's" William F. Buckley. Buckley would host more than 1,400 episodes of "Firing Line," until he gave it up in 1999. He was credited with putting conservatism (not just Republicanism) back on the table in American political discourse and with inspiring generations of young conservatives. Witty, acerbic, lethal in debate and with an unmatched arsenal of words, over the years Buckley made several stops in Kansas City beginning in 1975 when he taped two "Firing Line" programs at the old Multimedia Forum at Crown Center.

To supplement its national programming schedule, KCPT bought such syndicated programs as "Captain Kangaroo" and "The Lawrence Welk Show." The captain, whose marsupial name came from the big pockets in his coats, was played by Bob Keeshan as a tribute to the often-warm relationship between grandparents and grandchildren. "Lawrence Welk," as everyone knew, paired top-tier musicianship with, in the words of one critic, "some of the squarest music on the planet." But people were captivated by Welk's smooth manner, his struggles with the English idiom, his Champagne Ladies and, of course, his trademark count-off, "A one and a two ... ."

One of the city's major annual charity events, the Bacchus Ball, that year benefited KCPT.

A new station publication, *KCPT Magazine,* replaced the *KCPT Program Guide* in October 1989. It was larger and glossier and for the first time included advertising. A column by John Masterman noted that "Kansas City Illustrated" was beginning its seventh season and commented:

(Continued on page 79)

The Champagne Music of Lawrence Welk

March 12, 1992

To the Devoted Fans of the Lawrence Welk Show
at KCPT Public Television 19:

What can I say? I was so touched by the mammoth Birthday card you sent, with the names of all you nice people. To think you cared enough to call in is one of the nicest birthday gifts I've ever received. May I express my heartfelt thanks for your kindness to all of you who supported our show so generously.

With every good wish and a truly big thank you from this old music man!

Musically yours,

Lawrence Welk

Many Kansas City viewers were enthusiastic Lawrence Welk fans and the maestro returned the compliment.

KCPT was the beneficiary of one of Kansas City's stellar charity galas, the Bacchus Ball.

It is difficult to produce a television documentary that is both incisive and probing when every 12 minutes one is interrupted by 12 dancing rabbits singing about toilet paper.

– ROD SERLING,
television producer and creator of "The Twilight Zone"

(*Continued from page 76*)

Most of us associated with "Kansas City Illustrated" dealt with immediate events as reporters at commercial TV stations. The thing we longed for then was time – time to report stories thoroughly, meaningfully. "Kansas City Illustrated" has given us that time.

Kansas native Jim Lehrer returned frequently to lend his presence to events.

In January 1990, the Southwestern Bell Telephone Company installed an entirely new telephone system at the station free of charge. Talk about community support!

Public television's most recognizable personality arguably was Jim Lehrer, a Kansas native and University of Missouri journalism school graduate. Lehrer had maintained a special interest in KCPT even after becoming co-anchor of a nightly news program that had become a national habit. He attended a May 1990 luncheon for program underwriters and potential donors to the capital campaign. That same month, "Kansas City Illustrated" picked up two Kansas City Press Club awards. One was for a report on crack babies and the other for the "Gettysburg of the West," a photographic essay on the Civil War Battle of Westport, much of it fought in what is now Kansas City's Loose Park.

The show "The Miracle Planet" premiered as part of a public television nationwide environmental effort titled "Operation Earth." Locally, KCPT produced 50,000 copies of a popular booklet: *101 Things You Can Do to Save the Environment.* A two-hour environmental program produced jointly with KMBC-TV's Channel 9 won a Mid-America Regional Emmy award, its first regional Emmy. David Welsh and John Masterman produced the program. During the annual auction that year, KCPT offered free tree saplings provided by the Missouri Department of Conservation. CAB took a particular interest in the environmental project, which included many other KCPT conservation activities.

A note to a PT 19 financial statement revealed significant donations to the capital fund drive from the Hall Family Foundation, the Yellow Freight Foundation, the Francis Family Foundation, the William T. Kemper Foundation and the Courtney S. Turner Charitable Trust.

It was a necessary evil to interrupt regular programming for pledge-night pitches, a practice that continued to irritate even the most loyal viewers. The loss of part of an "Andy Williams Christmas Special" so inflamed a Channel 19 member that he immediately canceled his KCPT membership, and he was not alone. In a

Channel 19 was a regular in the annual downtown St. Patrick's Day parade.

(Continued from page 81)
It marked the beginning of a year in which the station emphasized activities supporting families, schools and community service.

Strong community support continued. A February 1991 report by Karen Kraft and her co-workers included news of KCPT's popular St. Patrick's Day Parade float and brisk ticket sales for a Sonoma County wine-tasting event to benefit the station at the Hyatt Regency Hotel.

In May 20, KCPT broadcast a Randy Mason documentary about artist George Caleb Bingham's hometown, the village of Arrow Rock, Mo., and its successful Lyceum Theatre.

The March subscription drive had set an all-time record, with responses during "Civil War" rebroadcasts accounting for much of the success.

In June, a KCPT endowment fund was established, to be administered by the Greater Kansas City Community Trusts and Foundations.

On Sept. 9, in anticipation of Bob Fuzy's retirement, William T. Reed took control of operations as executive vice president and general manager. A decorated Vietnam veteran, Reed came to KCPT from PBS, where he was a senior vice president as well as a consultant to CPB. His experience and friendships at that level would serve Channel 19 well.

On Sept. 29, 1991, KCPT celebrated its 30th anniversary with an afternoon party in the studios and parking lot and on the air. The celebrants included Mr. McFeeley of PBS's "Mr. Rogers Neighborhood," the Purple Panda, Kansas City's Marching Cobras, clowns and musical groups. Mayor (later U.S. Rep.) Emmanuel Cleaver was in attendance to proclaim "KCPT Day."

KCPT was selected to participate in the Sesame Street Preschool Education Project (PEP) to help teachers in day-care centers encourage reading readiness. A Kansas City Junior League grant funded the purchase of PEP materials. The program was conceived by PBS chairman Ralph B. Rogers, a co-founder of Children's Television Workshop, after studies indicated that two-thirds of all preschool children would have mothers in the work force by 1995.

On Oct. 1, Bill Reed was elected president of Public Television 19. A plaque from the officers and directors expressed their appreciation to Bob Fuzy for his 19 years at the helm, a tenure that had seen the PT 19 annual budget grow from $250,000 to $5 million.

One of the new president's policies was to respond in writing to letters addressed to him, and voluminous correspondence files would be part of Reed's legacy. His letters reflect endless patience, tenacity and diplomacy. His first message to viewers in the 1992 KCPT Program Guide expressed the conviction that

Bob Fuzy retired after 19 years at the station's helm.

PBS Senior Vice President Bill Reed came on board.

Mayor Emmanuel Cleaver came to KCPT's 30th anniversary party.

"local programming and station outreach activities are the most important services we can provide to communities in our coverage area."

At year-end, KCPT introduced a new Guide to Kansas City Public Television to major supporters and community leaders. It was much more informative than *KCPT Magazine*. "In my opinion," Reed said, "KCPT is an undervalued and under-funded Kansas City institution, and the guide is critically important in beginning our efforts to change this current situation."

Channel 19 had the jazz scene — historic and current — covered.

In February 1992, the Channel 19 program "Swingin' the Blues – Goin' to Kansas City" recalled the city's proud jazz heritage as part of the observance of Black History Month. That program was followed by the story of baseball in the Negro Leagues, with a great title: "Only the Ball was White."

In August, PBS (Robert MacNeil) and NBC (Tom Brokaw) joined forces to cover the Republican and Democratic National Conventions instead of offering separate, repetitive gavel-to-gavel coverage. *Los Angeles Times* Pulitzer Prize-winning TV critic Howard Rosenberg labeled it a "historic cost-cutting venture" and allowed there was still plenty of TV coverage for the nominating conventions that have been "light-on-news, heavy-on-image events for years, and there will be no exceptions in 1992."

Another Mark Russell fundraiser at the Folly Theater in September was a sellout. (The Spencer, Fane law firm bought 460 seats.) Russell's "Campaign Specials" on Fridays in September that election year looked back with amusement at previous presidential campaigns.

On Oct. 2, John Masterman's "Kansas City Week in Review," with KCPT's Deborah Holmes and veteran radio talk-show (KCKN) host Mike Shanin, appeared on Channel 19, covering events in the greater Kansas City area.

Assisted by a three-year federal grant, KCPT introduced the "GED on TV" series. This graduate equivalent degree program received an important boost when, through the good offices of PT 19 director Marjorie Grant, American Multi-Cinema provided two weeks' public service time for the series on 60 AMC screens throughout the Kansas City metro area. It was a significant community service that became an important rehabilitation resource for the Missouri Division of Probation and Parole.

"Barney and Friends" made its debut on Channel 19 in November. A purple anthropomorphic Tyrannosaurus rex, Barney was conceived by a Dallas mother looking for something that would interest her son. She and her team created a series of home videos that were shown locally. After the character was revamped, it was picked up by PBS for viewers age 2 to 5. It was interactive and play-oriented, encouraging preschoolers to participate. It also was an unexpected success – PBS had acquired the program to fill a temporary schedule gap and planned to replace it but reconsidered when millions of kids quickly adopted Barney.

Gamma Phi Beta sorority had for several years sponsored a popular antique show. With the aid of a grant from the William T. Kemper Foundation, KCPT joined

From left, auction chairwoman Joyce Kemp, auction coordinator Karen Rankin and KCPT president and general manager Robert Fuzy show off items to be sold at the April 1992 auction.

KCPT Magazine highlighted PBS/NBC's joint political convention coverage.

the sorority as co-sponsor and the enterprise was expanded to include a garden show. The Great Gardening Symposium Silent Garden Auction and Reception was staged at the Ritz Carleton ballroom in January 1993.

HOT POTATO: 'IN THE LIFE'

"IN THE LIFE," a series produced by New York's WNYC-TV about issues important to Kansas City's gay and lesbian community, premiered on KCPT on Jan. 4, 1993. There were a great many reactions, both pro and con. That came as no surprise. The monthly broadcasts, deliberately scheduled at the late hour of 10:30 p.m., were preceded by warnings about the adult nature of the program. Bill Reed responded gratefully to a supportive letter:

> *Your letter is the second nice letter received today about "IN THE LIFE" – an upbeat way to end the week; thanks.*
>
> *I am sorry to say that your observations are pretty much on target; we have received numerous very abusive telephone calls this past week (which is one of the reasons your letter gives us all a lift around here).*

In a Feb. 10, 1993, update, Reed wrote, "Receiving comments, letters, both pro and con (about even) on IN THE LIFE." This continued to be the case in ensuing months, even after the broadcast time was changed to midnight.

A few years later, in 1997, Reed received a leadership award from GLADD (the Gay and Lesbian Alliance Against Defamation) for his persistence. The presenter was the daughter of Sonny Bono and Cher, Chastity Bono, who in 2009 underwent female-to-male reassignment surgery and in 2010 a legal name change

Auction volunteers.

A phone bank.

Feeding the volunteers.

to Chaz. KCPT continues to offer a monthly late-hour broadcast of "IN THE LIFE."

Letters to all of the Kansas City area TV stations requesting simulcast time during the 1993 Auction included the following:

> *According to the other PTV stations across the country, the rapport KCPT has with the other television stations in the Kansas City area is unique, and we are very proud of that. Your support adds greatly to our success. Our records reflect a significant increase in bidding during the simulcast time. This in turn increases the overall success of our auction.*

The request for simulcasts was granted. George Powell noted in his biography, *The Sky is the Limit*, that beginning with the first auction, "the commercial stations boost the Annual Auction and volunteer some of their personalities to help out."

The 1993 auction set a new record, $375,737 (the goal was $325,000). A one-day group charter trip to the Indianapolis 500 was one of the more popular auction items, and a Helzberg diamond ring brought $2,100.

The capital campaign appeared to have bogged down – with only $2.2 million of its $5 million goal attained – despite a grant from the H&R Block Foundation.

An auction was a complex organism requiring leadership, hundreds of volunteers and a skilled crew.

But it got new life in April 1993, buoyed by the prospect of a $100,000 grant from the Kresge Foundation, as well as contributions from the Shirley and Barnett Helzberg and the Sosland foundations.

Attorney Charles Horner explained his gift as he presented KCPT with a check for $10,000, a bequest by his mother, Alma Louise Dallas Robinson:

> *She was a long-time fan of KCPT and enjoyed the educational and cultural programs ... particularly the "MacNeil/Lehrer News Hour," "Washington Week in Review," "Wall Street Week" and "Masterpiece Theatre."*

According to "Quality Time," a 1993 report by the Twentieth Century Fund Task Force on Public Television:

> *Public television's instructional programming has been popular with teachers from the beginning because almost all of it is custom-made and curriculum driven ... As a producer of instructional programming, the public television community has no peer.*

Auction MC Dana Hickam with a friend.

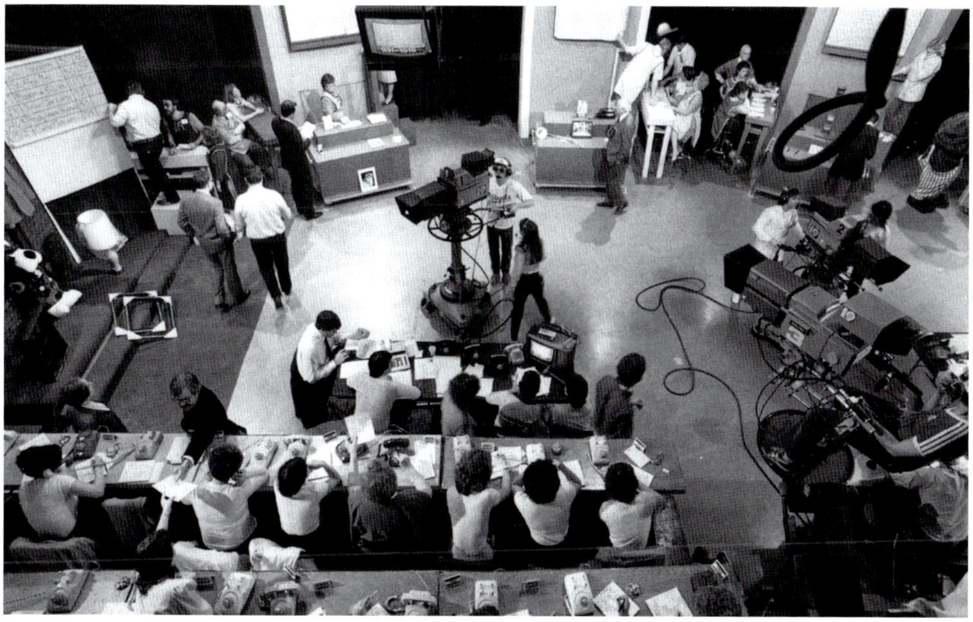

Auction economics: This night there were 2,500 items for auction and supporters hoped it would raise 12 percent of the station's operating budget.

Writer Charles Gusewelle has collaborated on many projects with KCPT.

Gas Service Company executive Tom Hall succeeded William Skelly as PT 19 chairman at the October 1993 annual meeting.

Popular *Kansas City Star* columnist Charles Gusewelle was the American leader of a joint U.S.- Russian 2,700 mile expedition beginning at the Siberian source of Russia's Lena River. Gusewelle and his party returned with more than 57 hours of video. He had spent over a decade negotiating and planning for the trip.

Efforts to interest commercial stations in a documentary went nowhere, but a chance social encounter with Bill Reed brought Gusewelle to KCPT. The station produced a 90-minute documentary, "A Great Current Running." Edited by Mike Murphy, it premiered on Oct. 27, 1993. KCPT's association with Gusewelle became an enduring relationship, to the great benefit of the station and its viewers.

BACK IN THE FRYING PAN: 'TALES OF THE CITY'

Another public relations hot potato was "Tales of the City," based on the first of American author Armistead Maupin's series of eight novels about San Francisco in the 1970s. *The New York Times* had described the 1978 novel as "an extended love letter to a magical San Francisco." First serialized in the *San Francisco Chronicle*, it was very much a chronicle of the times, with interrelated characters and plots and nonjudgmental depiction of recreational drug use and openly homosexual relationships. The January 1994 airing, part of PBS's "American Playhouse" series, was a major television event with very high viewership ratings.

By all accounts, telephones rang off the hook at public TV stations across the country. In Kansas City, the program produced a record number of responses both pro and con. Seventy-five KCPT members canceled their memberships, and there was criticism from some members of Congress and ammunition for those who wanted to eliminate all federal funding for public television. At a public hearing of the Corporation for Public Broadcasting, the Family Research Council's Robert Knight called it "a slick piece of gay propaganda."

Bill Reed discussed with callers the rationale for airing the program, one of whom remained unconvinced:

> *Dear Mr. Reed:*
>
> *Thank you, very much, for taking the time to discuss "Tales of the City" and explain why you chose to air the program. You gave a plausible explanation for making the decision to do so. Perhaps if all viewers exhibited your mature assessment of the merits of*

(Continued on page 91)

Charles Gusewelle wrote where he could on the U.S.-Russian Lena River expedition. The result was a book and the documentary "A Great Current Running."

John Jordan "Buck" O'Neil, center, talks baseball with KCPT's Randy Mason and Victor Hogstrom.

(Continued from page 88)

> *the plot it might be justifiable. I still question the wisdom of PBS sponsoring programs that need a warning. If it is that type of program let someone else show it.*
>
> *It seems to me that an important part of education and entertainment is displaying good taste. It starts in the home (which now days means television), the schools and the media. I would hope that PBS would be the standard bearer for this cause.*
>
> *Thanks.*

President and CEO Bill Reed lobbied for a sequel to "Tales of the City."

Undaunted, Reed lobbied the producers, urging them to do a sequel, and when this did not materialize, unsuccessfully tried to organize a group of stations to fund a sequel without PBS. His faith later was justified by a Peabody Award, the most prestigious in broadcasting.

The subjects of other programs were more mundane, as represented by this appreciative letter from a Lawson, Mo., viewer:

> *I would like to say thanks for the fine programming on KCPT. If it weren't for you, my TV would likely be in the trash. All the wood-shop and gardening shows are my favorites. My wife loves watching all the cooking shows. I am waiting anxiously for a new season of the "New Yankee Workshop."*

Kansas City Monarchs' first baseman and manager Buck O'Neil became the first black coach in the Major Leagues.

KEN BURNS MEETS BUCK O'NEIL

In September, 1994, more than 43 million people watched the PBS documentary miniseries "Baseball" – another Ken Burns triumph, topping his "The Civil War" as the most watched program in the 25-year history of the network. KCPT followed with its own celebrated documentary on the Negro Leagues, "Ain't Seen Nothing Like It Since – The Kansas City Monarchs," produced by KCPT's Teddy Dibble.

In preparation for the September debut of "Baseball" and its "Monarchs" chaser, Ken Burns visited Kansas City in August for a Royals-Oakland baseball game. The Royals wore Kansas City Monarchs uniforms, and the Monarch's John Jordan "Buck" O'Neil caught Burns' first pitch. Buck, the Monarchs' first baseman and manager, had gone on to become the first black coach in the Major Leagues. The Burns documentary was the station's highest-rated program of the year, with the genial O'Neil in a starring role.

Countless national interviews and awards followed for Buck, the unofficial goodwill spokesman for the Negro Leagues. He joked that he was "an overnight

Let's face it, there are no plain women on television.
– ANNA FORD,
British broadcaster

"KC Crossroads" profiled KC's Queen Bey.

sensation at 82." President George W. Bush later awarded him, posthumously, the nation's highest civilian honor, the Presidential Medal of Freedom. The Baseball Hall of Fame created the Buck O'Neil Lifetime Achievement Award and erected a Buck O'Neil statue in Cooperstown, N.Y. (A Royals game in July 1995 honored Buck during pregame festivities that included showing part of the Monarchs documentary on the ballpark's giant Jumbotron.)

On the occasion of Buck's 100th birthday anniversary Nov. 13, 2011, a *Kansas City Star* headline declared that Buck "chose joy over anger," illustrated by this quote: "Waste no tears for me. I didn't come along too early. I was right on time."

Another memorable quote: "Son, in this life you don't ever walk by a red dress."

"K.C. Biznet," a 30-minute KCPT production that covered local business news, profiled Kansas City Power & Light CEO Drew Jennings. It was funded by the Mason Dean Charitable Trust.

The burden of producing "Marquee" weekly became too great, and to the regret of its many fans it was rescheduled as a monthly program supplemented by "Extras." The first Extra, in 1994, featured the handsome new Kemper Museum of Contemporary Art.

In October 1994, KCPT produced "KC Crossroads," an hour-long program spotlighting area jazz and blues talent. One performer, Karrin Allyson, was a favorite at Kansas City's Grand Emporium, one of America's best blues clubs. (A Nov. 6, 1996, *Wall Street Journal* article described her as "one of the best young jazz singers around" – one who "could waltz into any New York nightclub and tear up the joint.") Another performer, Queen Bey, was a product of Kansas City's legendary Orchid Room. She was inducted into the Elder Statesmen of Kansas City Jazz and known as Kansas City's Ambassador of Jazz.

BECOMING A TELECOMMUNICATIONS HUB

In 1994, KCPT spent more than $600,000 on national programming. At the same time, the station was evolving from a broadcast operation to a telecommunications center.

It had a new online interactive telecommunications system, LINK 19, used by teachers and students; it had managed the hospital services component of American Cablevision's Institutional Network (I-NET) since its inception; and it had other nonbroadcast distribution technologies, including Instructional Television Fixed Services (ITFS), satellite up-linking and videotape distribution. It worked with the Kansas City Public Library in telecommunication and had a long relationship with American Cablevision. It wanted to manage I-NET for

(Continued on page 94)

Karrin Allyson, another "KC Crossroads" profile, was often described as one of the country's best young jazz singers.

(Continued from page 92)
the entire community, as well as operate a full-time children's (K-12) channel for American Cablevision. The interest in electronic alternatives was almost clairvoyant and continues.

From time to time, there were criticisms of PBS's nature programming – too much graphically portrayed violence, reproduction, etc. (One Channel 19 viewer objected to "simply too much fins, feathers and fowl programming.") However, the telecasts attracted large audiences and financial support. Evelyn Abrams died March 1, 1994, leaving $10,000 to KCPT "to continue to enhance programming in the area of nature in accordance with the examples set by 'Nature and Wild America' aired on KCPT."

NATURE®

PBS' stunning nature programming didn't please everyone.

Kansas City was one of 10 national sites selected to hold workshops for teachers offered by the National Teacher Training Institute for Science, Television and Technology, a partnership of KCPT with PBS flagship station WNET/NY, CPB and Texaco. There was a $10,000 grant to the station from Texaco for the workshop.

A June 1994 letter addressed to "KCPT and Each and Every Sponsor of the National Teacher Training Institute" began: "Thank you! You gave us a wonderful two days packed full of ideas, technology and practical applications for our teaching!"

It ended: "Thank you, Thank you! – for free tuition plus an inspirational two days."

The station received uncounted letters of gratitude:

My class enjoyed the fold-out dinosaur book you sent.

My 6-year-old son, 2-year-old daughter and myself enjoy the "Storytime" show very much. The variety of books this show offers is terrific. I read to my children and we visit the library but it is great to have the change of pace "Storytime" offers.

For 25 years I taught social studies at Shawnee Mission West. I used to tape portions of "MacNeil-Lehrer," "Washington Week" and "Wall Street Week" for use with my students. I even had a class slogan – TGFML (Thank God for "MacNeil-Lehrer.")

John Masterman, in fragile health, was approaching retirement, and in August, Cynthia Smith, well known to Kansas City viewers as nightly anchor and reporter for WDAF-TV news, came to KCPT as director of community affairs and vice president for corporate communications. Masterman retired Oct. 1, 1994, and moved to Tucson, Ariz., where he died in 1999. His death was much mourned in Kansas City – his documentaries and other journalistic contributions had served KCPT well.

Smith, an Emmy winner and founder of the TV-4 Love Fund for Children, was a good fit for KCPT, where she would handle advertising, public relations, promotions, community affairs and viewer information.

An October letter from an Independence viewer was candid in its criticism of "Au Revoir" – "don't show it again, with all the filthy dialog." But the writer praised several other programs, and in the end was forgiving. After asking pardon for the typing ("it's one finger now since a stroke"), the letter concluded:

> *"I'm glad we have KCPT."*

One writer said: "Three cheers for you and your excellent – and much needed – programs. I am especially grateful for 'I'll Fly Away.'" But another had reservations: "I'm glad you are rerunning 'I'll Fly Away,' if all the almost nude sex episodes have been removed."

In December, one S. Mohammed, professing to represent "a particular group of UMKC students," wrote to protest against a PBS documentary "Jihad in America," charging that it was based on ignorance of Islam in general and jihad in particular. A letter from Bill Reed disputed the charge of bias and identified a noted Muslim authority on Islamic fundamentalism as part of the PBS production staff.

Another December letter was poignant and rewarding:

> *Just a kind word to say how much my husband and I watched KCPT. Mike passed away a few months back but I now watch with tears in my eyes. You have so many good programs. I wish I could do more to help.*

WDAF anchor and reporter Cynthia Smith came to KCPT.

Television brought the brutality of war into the comfort of the living room.
Vietnam was lost in the living rooms of America — not on the battlefields of Vietnam.

— MARSHALL McLUHAN,
known for the phrase "the medium is the message,"
considered by many the leading prophet of the electronic age

Bill Nye, whose set was called "Nye Labs," was likened to a modern "Mr Wizard."

KANSAS CITY was selected as one of the pilot communities for PBS' new "Ready to Learn" series, directed at the home environment for home-bound, at-risk children ages 2 to 12. The nine-hour daily program began in January 1995 with a grant from the Courtney S. Turner Charitable Trust. Kids Television 19, with 11 consecutive hours of children's programs, also debuted.

In addition to the long time favorites ("Sesame Street," "Barney" and "Mister Rogers"), there were "The Puzzle Place," with puppets showing preschoolers the value of diversity, and "Bill Nye the Science Guy," aimed at science-ready preteens. Nye, dressed in a blue lab coat and bow tie, mixed serious science with action, humor and special effects. It was early geek hip. Most episodes featured a mock song and music video related to the topic of the day – for example, an episode on cells featured Mighty Chondria singing "Cellular Haze," a parody of Jimi Hendrix's "Purple Haze."

That same month the William T. Kemper Foundation funded a new half-hour program, "Ruckus," moderated by Mike Shanin. Billed as "a spirited discussion of the issues among people who agree to disagree" and patterned after the contentious PBS "McLaughlin Group" concept, it came under fire almost at once from conservatives and liberals alike for "loud and obnoxious debates."

There was a general plea to "let the national media do this job." But Bill Reed stood fast, declaring his intent to give the show more time, "so we can find the right format and the right mix of people who can shine light from several directions on the issues, with a little humor along the way."

In 1995, with national elections pending, federal funding of public broadcasting came under fire again. A Shawnee Mission School District teacher admonished one of the Congressional proponents of "zeroing out" government support: "Killing off the system that produced 'Sesame Street' is the psychological equivalent of killing Bambi. How could you?" And a Kansas City, Kan., attorney, in response to efforts to cut funding for public TV, wrote to KCPT and Topeka's public station KTWU that his son learned to recognize letters at the age of 1 and to read at age 2 "because he watched Sesame Street completely and thoroughly on a daily basis."

Gamma Phi Beta sorority presented KCPT with a check for $5,000 from the 1994 "Kansas City Antiques and Garden Show," and another $5,000 gift in June. The sorority had been a loyal KCPT supporter for 17 years and the constant underwriter of "Mister Rogers' Neighborhood." The Garden Show money was designated, and used, for the Sesame Street Preschool Education Project. The collaboration continued for many years, growing revenues and benefitting KCPT.

The items offered in the 1995 auction included an Italian greyhound, which prompted a critical letter to the editor in *The Kansas City Star* from a dog lover. In response, Bill Reed pointed out that the same day there were 228 ads in *The Star* touting dogs for sale. However, there were enough complaints that a "no dogs or cats" policy was adopted for future auctions. KCPT would make amends to its canine friends by airing "Dog's Best Friend," underwritten by the Kansas City Veterinary Association, and "Woof! A Guide to Dog Training," underwritten by Pet Food Savemart.

One year the station's list of items for auction included an Italian greyhound. Never again.

As of May 1, 1995, "GED on TV" had produced 54 Missouri graduates, an estimated 31 in Kansas, and the Missouri Department of Corrections was preparing to expand its participation in the program for prisoners and parolees.

In June, KCPT joined with John Knox Village in Lee's Summit to present Lawrence Welk's Myron Floren and the UMKC Accordian Orchestra in concert at the village. More than 1,200 enthusiastic Welk fans attended the benefit performance and danced the polka to Floren's tunes.

Attorney Daniel C. Weary became PT 19 chairman in 1995.

At the 1995 annual meeting, prominent attorney Daniel C. Weary (Husch Blackwell) succeeded Tom Hall as PT 19 chairman. Weary and the Bank of America had been very supportive of KCPT as co-trustees of the Courtney S. Turner Charitable Trust, and he offered wise counsel as a member of the PT 19 board. He also recruited David Francis for the board, to continue the Francis family's interest and support.

RARELY HAD THERE BEEN A VISION SO ASTUTE FOR A SHOW

In the fall, Randy Mason and Mike Murphy picked up cameraman Don Mayberger in Lawrence, Kan., and set out on an off-the-highway tour of Kansas grassroots art and roadside attractions. When Mayberger asked, "What's the plan?" they had to confess that there was none. But the resulting program, "Rare Visions and Roadside Revelations," was applauded by viewers (200 calls), won the Kansas City Press Club's award for best documentary, and earned a regional Emmy nomination. The coveted Emmys, of course, are awarded by the National Academy of Television Arts and Sciences to recognize excellence in television. They are to television what the Oscars are to film. While not as sweeping as a national Emmy, regional awards are hotly contested and convey significant prestige.

Outsider art: J. L. Nippers' "Statue of Liberty."

The weasels carved the country into five digestible chunks for this Kansas City Star book.

For Mason and Murphy, "Rare Visions" was a lark in the country, a welcome change from the pressures of producing "Marquee," and it challenged a recent ranking of the state of Kansas as last in the country for tourist attractions. The emphasis was on fun, and the crew dubbed themselves "the weasels" because of their ability to weasel their way into places in search of a story.

"Rare Visions" originally was intended to be a single program, but the unexpected acclaim prompted a one-year series. That "one-year series" has been extended, year after year. The show has since been recognized with multiple regional Emmy awards, is syndicated to PBS stations around the country and is distributed for broadcast on Indonesian television.

Producer Pam James was a new hire at KCPT in 1995, a lapsed child of public television who had been lured away by cable: "My first day at KCPT, I had the pleasure of sitting through the screening of the very first 'Rare Visions and Roadside Revelations.' I knew I had found where I belonged." Pam was followed a month later by Angee Simmons, another public TV apostate who got her foot in the door as a KCPT pledge drive volunteer and found her calling there as a producer of note.

Responses to solicitations were usually checks, without comment. But one recently widowed woman wrote to explain that she had been unable to answer a pledge plea until her pension arrived. Now it had, and "this check to you is the first one written" — the widow's mite.

On Jan. 17, 1996, a new KCPT education division was formed: MoKan Kids' Network, a name proposed by Chairman Weary. It was a separate legal entity to advance instructional TV. Its chairman, vice chairman and secretary were educators from, respectively, the Shawnee Mission, Blue Springs and Bonner Springs school districts. By the following June, there were 208 school district members in the Network's ITV service and 18 in its online service. One year later, there were 342 school districts, including (after years of wooing) the Kansas City, Mo., district.

The Ready to Learn program benefitted on Feb. 14 from a Valentine's Day campaign involving the sale of "I Am Loved" stuffed animals, shirts, balloons and golf balls at kiosks in selected shopping centers. The Shirley and Barnett Helzberg Foundation initiated the campaign. The "I Am Loved" trademark was created by Barnett Helzberg for the Helzberg family jewelry business in the '60's when Shirley agreed to marry him.

(Continued on page 103)

Road warriors Mike Murphy, Randy Mason and Don Mayberger let nothing stand in the way of their quest for the scenic, the quirky and the just plain nuts.

"Rare Visions & Roadside Revelations" has won 12 regional Emmy Awards.

(Continued from page 100)

"I Am Loved" buttons got worldwide distribution. A soldier in Vietnam quoted in *The Kansas City Times*, wrote: "I pinned one on a sour old sergeant. It's the first time I've seen him smile since we got here."

When Barnett Helzberg sold the business to tycoon Warren Buffet, the Helzberg Foundation retained the rights to the trademark and later transferred it free of charge to Helzberg Diamonds.

Helzberg told *The Kansas City Times*' Matt Campbell: "Television is an incredibly powerful teaching force and TV 19 has really committed to being kids' TV. One hundred percent of the daytime programming is children's TV. That's an incredible gift to the community."

As part of the March 1996 membership drive, KCPT aired a new local production by Jack Cashill of *Ingram's Magazine*: "Remember Me, KC." The documentary was created from interviews of Kansas Citians living on August 7, 1951, and employed biographical sketches to portray everyday lives in Kansas City at that

The "I Am Loved" trademark ...

... was created in the '60s by Barnett Helzberg when Shirley agreed to marry him.

Bill Reed was inducted into the Silver Circle of the National TV Academy and the weasels were honored at an awards occasion in St. Louis, Mo. From left, Dee Rusconi, Tari Hodges, Mary Anne Reed, Don Mayberger, Bill Reed, Randy Mason and Mike Murphy.

KCPT aired Jack Cashill's "Remember Me, KC."

W. Jackson Letts succeeded Dan Weary as PT 19 board chairman.

time. Why that date? Cashill says he wanted to pivot the story on the national transition from a railroad to an airplane culture, and two pertinent things happened here on Aug. 7, 1951:

> *Baseball great Jackie Jensen came by train to KC to play for the KC Blues. His career would be curtailed by his fear of flying. Also, Norman Rockwell flew into town that day to be commissioned to paint the iconic "KC spirit" painting in the wake of the 1951 flood, which also crippled rail travel.*

At the 1996 PT 19 annual meeting, W. Jackson Letts was elected chairman, following Dan Weary. Also, a new member of the Board, Michael Carter, had credentials familiar to those with memories of the station's formative years. His resume stated:

> *Michael Carter is a Kansas City native, and president and general manager of KPRS. Started by his grandfather "Skip" Carter, KPRS is the oldest African-American owned radio station west of the Mississippi.*

KCPT formed a partnership with a California organization, Store of Knowledge, which opened a store on Kansas City's Country Club Plaza in the fall of 1996. It sold learning and reference materials for schoolteachers and home use. The Plaza store was its eighth location in the country, each affiliated with a local public television station. By mid-October the store's daily sales averaged $7,000. KCPT had no monetary investment in the project but granted the store the right to use its name and logo, and provided promotional support, in return for a percentage of the profits.

KCPT also raised money by offering production services to non-profit companies. The new eight-person department directed by Chip Tate produced public service announcements for Missouri Safe Schools and a campaign to make the public aware of programs available to youth. (Before becoming director, Tate was nominated for a regional Emmy for his musical composition "5 'til 4," the theme song for KCPT's "Marquee" show.)

The indefatigable Bill Reed was elected to the boards of directors of the highly respected American Public Television Stations (APTS) and the Southern Education Communications Association (SECA), and chaired the Kansas Public Broadcasting Council.

Channel 19 teamed with a new Plaza shop, The Store of Knowledge.

In May 1997, Randy Mason and Mike Murphy edited and produced an ambitious documentary, "This Place Called Home," written and narrated by reporter-poet Charles Gusewelle. It required several months to produce. Not underwritten, it was a gamble in which KCPT invested a precious $42,000. The station ran ads asking for material from the city's past. That brought walk-in contributors to the station with old photographs, home movies and reminiscences offering a poignant look at how things were, from the summer heat and the neighborhood movie houses to the Great Depression and Boss Tom Pendergast. Kansas City cooks were invited by KCPT to contribute favorite recipes for a "This Place Called Home Cookbook," later offered for sale at the Store of Knowledge and local book stores. The program was a major success. It won a regional Emmy award.

Mason and Murphy fondly recall the contrast between Gusewelle pecking away on his old Royal typewriter and their use of a digital editing system to put the program together.

LOVE SONG TO A PLACE CALLED THE OZARKS

Gusewelle could use any instrument he wanted, having long before made an indelible mark on American journalism and letters. He left *The Kansas City Star* having been a reporter, editorial writer, foreign editor, associate editor and columnist (which he still is). Assignments had taken him to Latin America, Africa, the Middle East, Western and Eastern Europe and the former Soviet Union. For three years, he wrote his three-times-a-week *Star* column from France and Dakar,

Senegal. He wrote, at last count, 12 books, and would be back to add more heft to Channel 19's growing public profile.

KCPT protested in vain when Kansas City, Mo., awarded management of the K-12 educational access cable channel to the University of Missouri-Kansas City despite KCPT's 36 years of ITV experience.

Brian Gardner was elected board chairman in 1997.

In September, *The Kansas City Star* gave underwriting support to "Sesame Street" for the 20th consecutive year.

In October KCPT was inducted into the Mid-America Education Hall of Fame in recognition of its service to area students and their families. Brian Gardner succeeded W. Jackson Letts as PT 19 chairman, and Linda Graves, Kansas' First Lady, was elected to the board.

In late October, a new Ken Burns "Lewis and Clark" documentary was presented in Kansas City as part of the American Experience series. Narrated by Hal Holbrook, it traced the journey of the Corps of Discovery, the first exploration of the West by the United States.

Welk's Saturday night show had ended after 27 years but was resurrected in October on public television with selected programs dating from 1967. The response was enormous. A St. Joseph, Mo., viewer wrote that she was the same age as the maestro and: "I watch all the Lawrence Welk programs on TV. We listened to all his music when he started on radio in Yankton, S.D. ...We are old people and we sure like his program."

"To the Best of My Ability: The Story of Harry S. Truman" was a collaboration of KCPT with the National Park Service aimed at elementary school children. It featured three young local actors preparing a school report on President Truman, visiting libraries and archives and interviewing Clifton Truman Daniel, the president's grandson. It added one more instructional videotape program to the 1,600 distributed by the station across Missouri and Kansas or available at KCPT's lending library. As *The Star's* Brian Burnes wrote:

> *They call today's children the video generation. Harry S. Truman, by contrast, was born in the day of sepia-tone photographs.*
>
> *So, how do you introduce one to the other?*
>
> *With zippy music. With shaky, hand-held camera effects. With animation, even.*
>
> *The result is a 20-minute film on the 33rd president that's part documentary and part music video.*

The National Educational Telecommunications Association (NETA) recognized "To the Best of My Ability" as the best ITV production of the year. A copy was sent to the crew of the USS Harry S. Truman.

PBS introduced "Point of View" (POV). It would become public television's longest running showcase for independent nonfiction film. POV productions

(Continued on page 108)

In the editing studio, from left, Charles Gusewelle, Randy Mason and Mike Murphy use their tools of choice to put together "This Place Called Home."

"Point of View" is a powerful showcase for independent nonfiction film.

The POV documentary "Wo Ai Ni" (I Love You Mommy) ...

... tells the story of an 8-year-old orphan ...

... and the Long Island Jewish family that travels to China to adopt her.

(Continued from page 106)

would win every major film and broadcasting award, including 27 Emmys, 13 George Foster Peabody Awards, 10 Alfred I. duPont-Columbia Broadcast Journalism Awards, three Academy Awards and the Prix Italia. *USA Today* printed a typical critical evaluation:

> *So much of what we see is watered-down and easily digestible, designed to appeal to the largest common denominator and not cause offense. Against this pallid landscape of cream-puffery, POV stands out as something quite bright and unusual.*

GOING AFTER BIG BUCKS

The federal Balanced Budget Act of 1997 mandated a change that would set up one of those watershed moments to which everyone counted down. It required a changeover from the analog broadcasting standard, five decades old, to digital television (DTV) for both commercial and public TV. Public broadcasting stations would have to convert by 2003. The bill included $15 million to help fund the conversion.

As KCPT's program guide trumpeted: "The new digital age is coming, at once bedazzling and befuddling, rich with challenges and opportunities for Kansas City public television." KCPT had a wealth of programming available to it, but was restricted in its dissemination by the fact that only one broadcast channel was available —Channel 19.

Digital TV would allow broadcasting multiple programs simultaneously (multicasting) with enhanced picture and sound quality.

In 1997, in anticipation of the expense of conversion to digital, the KCPT board approved a new $10 million capital campaign to fund purchase of costly equipment and extensive renovation of station offices and facilities. It replaced the unfinished 1989 campaign; this need was more immediate. Youthful David Francis, 39, was appointed campaign co-chair, a major responsibility. Another, grayer co-chair was anticipated but when that failed to materialize Francis volunteered to go it alone, and plunged in with enthusiasm. In 1998, Mary Harris and John Francis accepted the role of honorary co-chairs. Board member Robert Bernstein of the Bernstein-Rein Advertising Agency was a valuable resource for the campaigners.

In April 1997, KCPT marked its 25th auction with the return of Mr. Bidmore. The penguin mascot had been missing from the show for several years when

"Paparazzi" auction volunteers, top row from left, Rudy Kuchan, Warren Kurtenbach, Mr. Bidmore, Art Moule and Bob Edmondson. Front row, Anne Kurtenbach, Mildred Kuchan and Ann Edmondson.

"The press" and "the bird" made a scene on the cover of KCPT Magazine.

John Francis was honorary co-chair of the 1997 capital campaign.

organizers decided to bring him back. To get the word out, volunteers dressed up as paparazzi on the trail of the illusive mascot.

On Nov. 7, 1998, installation of a new transmitter for digital broadcasting was completed and KCPT became the only broadcaster between Kansas City and the West Coast experimenting with digital TV. As a "Communique" from American Public Television Stations announced:

> *Seven public television stations were among the 40 stations in 23 cities in America that began broadcasting in digital in November. WETA, Washington, D.C.; KCTS, Seattle; KCPT, Kansas City; WITF, Harrisburg; WMVS/WMTV, Milwaukee; Oregon Public Broadcasting; and Mississippi Public Broadcasting premiered high-definition programming during PBS Digital Week, Nov. 9-12. All public television stations must convert to digital by May 2003.*

KCPT broadcast PBS's first experiment with "enhanced" digital television the night after the seven-station digital debut of which it was a part. As *The Star's* Aaron Barnhart wrote: "Public broadcasters are betting on digital to widen the mission of TV from something people watch into something they use." PBS named KCPT "A Pioneer in Digital Television."

(Continued on page 111)

An early cast of Ruckettes: From left, Steve Rose, Yael Abouhalkah, Mike Shanin, Rich Nadler and Trudy Hall.

(Continued from page 109)

The opening paragraph of Bob Bernstein's brochure for the capital campaign described the station:

> *Today, Kansas City Public Television serves over 856,000 people each month; educates 88,425 children each week during the day with the best non-violent, non-commercial, educational television programming available anywhere in the world; provides over 1,000 kids each month with their first book through KCPT's First Book Project; serves 344,000 kindergarten through 12th grade students and 27,000 teachers with on-line, instructional television and teacher training services each year throughout Missouri and Kansas; enrolls some 1,000 students each year for GED on TV and in five years 450 have received their equivalency degrees through this program; and provides the only regular in-depth local programming about the Greater Kansas City area with such programs as "Kansas City Week in Review," "Ruckus," "This Place Called Home," political debates and other specials.*

Barbara Nelson followed Brian Gardner as board chair.

The Department of Commerce's Public Telecommunications Program (PTEP) provided some matching grants for digital equipment and facilities. On Oct. 30, 1998, Missouri congressman Ike Skelton notified Bill Reed of a PTEP grant to facilitate the station's preparation for digital TV delivery and multi-channel service. The congressman characterized the grant as "quite an achievement" in light of the formidable competition for the funding.

At the October 1998 annual PT 19 board meeting, Barbara Nelson succeeded chairman Brian Gardner.

In November, the NETA convention brought 350 representatives of 85 stations from 38 states to Kansas City. They visited Buck O'Neil's Negro Leagues Museum and 18th and Vine for barbeque and jazz.

In December, "Ruckus" won the United Minority Media Association's "Time Well Spent" award. It was some vindication for Reed and his fortitude in the face of criticism of the program. (One viewer had written that the remarks of one of the panelists was "hateful, mean, degrading" and warned "rein him in" or risk losing viewers.)

Uncontroversial was a KCPT production of a Holiday Vespers Concert from the Lied Center of the University of Kansas in Lawrence.

Nick Haines, on the set of "Kansas City Week in Review," joined KCPT in June 1999.

(Continued from page 113)

SPOTLIGHT ON THE COMMUNITY

In June, the sharp, irrepressible Nick Haines joined the KCPT staff as executive producer of news and public affairs. He would host "Kansas City Week in Review," the weekly local news wrap-up previously produced by John Masterman, and also produce "Ruckus." Haines was a former BBC radio news reporter with a degree in government from Britain's University of Essex.

Later in June, KCPT hosted a town meeting that would become one segment in the three-hour prime time broadcast "Seeking Solutions," aired nationally Sept. 22. The Kansas City story involved residents of the Blue Hills neighborhood and their successful effort to shut down drug houses. The project was produced by PBS' Emmy Award-winning "Frontline" correspondent Hedrick Smith, who also had a Pulitzer for his work at *The New York Times*. The Kansas City segment was underwritten by the Ewing Marion Kauffman Foundation. City councilman and civic leader Alvin Brooks was among those interviewed.

As Smith told Barnhart: "What we're trying to do is show courageous, compelling examples of people coming up with solutions to violence in their communities."

In July 1999, a program called "It's Elementary," about child molestation, was very controversial. Angry responses, many of them incited by misrepresentations by a Mississippi minister, outnumbered the favorable ones. However, Bill Reed replied: "No matter what the tally, pro or con, the program was important to run, and KCPT will run it again in the future."

Reed saw lobbying legislators as part of his job. In August, he wrote to 40 Missouri state representatives, pointing out the services lost due to reduced funding for educational television. Only two responded. Undaunted, Reed repeated the exercise to solicit funding for child health programs from tobacco litigation settlement funds. He received an answer from a rural representative:

> *Your recent letter is exactly why funding for public television and radio is often endangered in the political process.*
>
> *Whether you and your liberal, country club, Junior League friends realize it or not, there are people who do not support assuaging your guilt over having a high salary by expending our tax dollars. Who will pay for government run health or day care for children when the tobacco settlement runs out? The taxpayers – that's who.*

David Francis chaired the capital campaign to raise $10 million for renovations and new digital equipment.

The Okayama bullet train station.

A young citizen of Kurashiki.

At the October 1999 annual meeting, David Francis succeeded Barbara Nelson as PT 19's chairman. A professional pilot who owned an airplane, Francis brought mobility to the KCPT management, on occasion making himself and his aircraft available to Reed, vice president for development and community partnerships Bonnie Rabicoff, and other staff members free of charge.

Another Reed effort, a meeting between him and the office of the Consulate General of Japan in Kansas City, led to a discussion of ways to promote better understanding between the peoples of the two countries. A major issue was the lack of current information in American schools about life in modern Japan.

After extensive arrangements with Japanese officials, KCPT sent a three-person documentary crew to Kurashiki — sister city to Kansas City — to videotape programs for presentation in U.S. schools.

For Channel 19 producer Pam James, Don the Cameraman (one of the "weasels") and Patricia Weiss of the University of Kansas Department of East Asian Studies, the 15-day trip began on the eve of their departure with dinner at the home of Consul General Tatsuo Tanaka and his wife. It ended at a banquet in their honor in Kurashiki where James gave a short speech in Japanese concluding memorably with a toast to *kaipan* (loin cloths) instead of *kampai* (long life).

(Continued on page 119)

Don't think it'll go in the overhead: *KCPT's Don Mayberger and Pam James flew business class on Japan Airlines.*

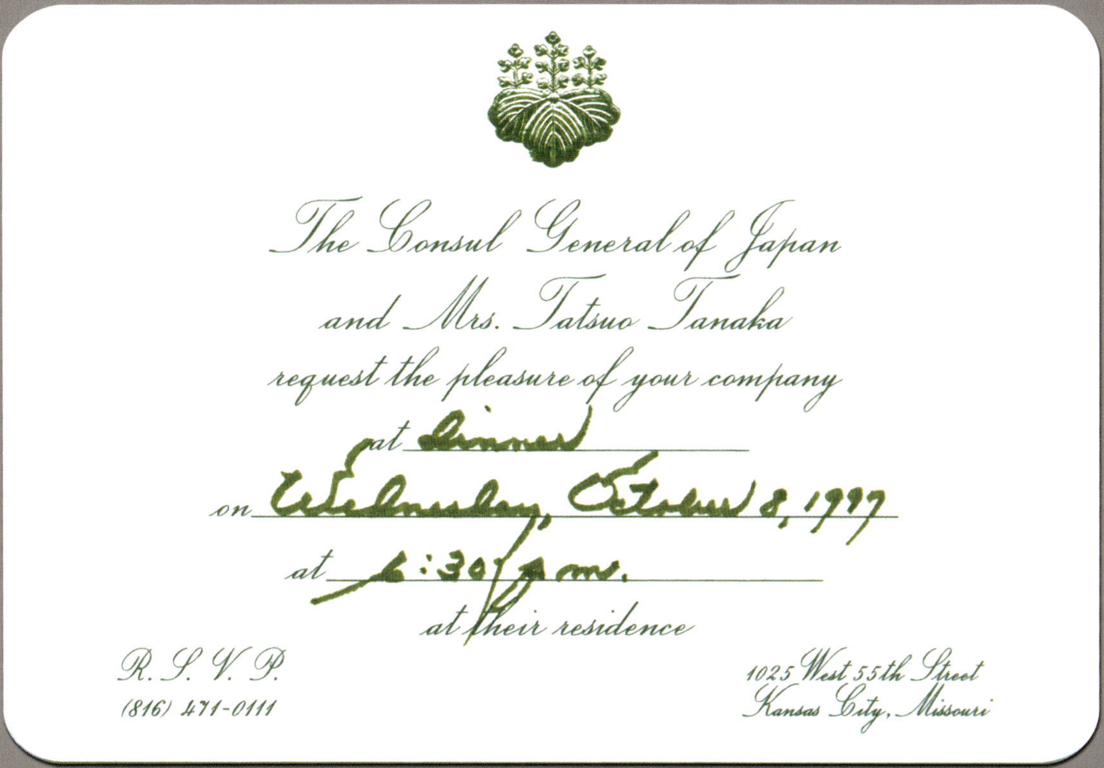
The Consul General of Japan
and Mrs. Tatsuo Tanaka
request the pleasure of your company
at dinner
on Wednesday, October 8, 1997
at 6:30 p.m.
at their residence

R. S. V. P.
(816) 471-0111

1025 West 55th Street
Kansas City, Missouri

Above, Yo Kurabayashi of International Motion Pictures Co., Inc., Pam James, Don Mayberger and KU's Patricia Weiss in Kurashiki. Top, invitation to dinner at the home of the Consul General of Japan and his wife the night before the trip.

Above, school-age children practice calligraphy. Top, the Heian Jingo Shrine in Kyoto.

(Continued from page 116)

In between, they took pictures and did interviews in the homes of two Kurashiki families; visited schools, stores, restaurants, rice and lotus farms; and stopped in Tokyo and Kyoto.

The result was a documentary, "Passport to Japan: Konnichawa" — Konnichawa being the Japanese greeting, "Good afternoon." The film was made for national distribution, and 57 public television stations in 17 states representing more than 8.8 million young people and their teachers signed up to televise it. It won first place in 1999 for Instructional Communications from NETA and a Distinguished Service Award for Academic Leadership from the International Relations Council.

It's not an exaggeration to say that millions of young people and their teachers gained a better understanding of life in Japan thanks to the combined efforts of the office of the Consulate General of Japan in Kansas City and a local public television station.

Back on the local front, on-air fund-raising continued to generate protest mail. A professional financial planner complained that "Once again, your station and your programming decision pre-empted the program 'Wall Street Week' from its normal time slot of 8:30 p.m. Friday to make room for a fund-raising auction program. I always watch 'Wall Street Week' on Friday evenings and I plan my schedule accordingly." Another viewer advised: "I'm always apprehensive when you (KCPT) have a pledge week. For at least three years that I can remember (maybe more) there is a screw-up at that time with programs that are a series ... The only way I've been able to get all the series has been a call to the program director to see when the omitted program will be found."

Critics usually were told that the drives generated essential dollars for KCPT and the hope was expressed that they could tolerate occasional interruptions. However, a detailed letter from one long-suffering Lawrence Welk fan deserved more than the customary response:

> *Last year you omitted showing Lawrence Welk TV show 11 times (March 6, 13, 20, April 17 & 24, May 22, June 26, Aug. 7, Nov. 27 & Dec. 11) and substituted 4 shows (June 19, Aug. 7, Nov. 27 and Dec. 4) from the Oklahoma Network schedule.*
>
> *On Dec. 4, you substituted the scheduled program to air "Lawrence Welk Songs of Faith," which you had previously substituted and aired 8/7/99. This was presented as a two hour show – one hour was made from Welk TV clips and a few 1999 performances by the Welk show hosts. The other hour was spent by the Welk show hosts,*

Viewers wanted the Lawrence Welk show and they wanted it when scheduled.

If something wasn't shown as scheduled, Bill Reed had the job of explaining why.

the Oklahoma network, KCPT announcers and guests begging everyone to make a pledge to keep the Lawrence Welk TV reruns on the air. No mention was made in that two-hour show that any of the money pledged during that time would be used for anything else.

You must have collected quite a bit of money during that two-hour show as the volunteers seemed busy on the telephones. Many probably made pledges to keep Lawrence Welk shows on TV – then to receive a slap in the face by KCPT when a week later (12/11/99) NO Welk show was aired! .... Let's keep the Welk show on the air every week.

Bill Reed had to admire the meticulous accounting and promised that an effort would be made to keep future Lawrence Welk interruptions to a minimum.

Occasionally, Reed's courtesy to critics was rewarded. One four-page, longhand letter declined membership renewal because of perceived liberal bias in public affairs programming. Reed's response pointed out the many other services rendered to the community by KCPT. Shortly thereafter, the membership was renewed, the writer explaining that his annoyance was caused by a perception of media bias in general rather than KCPT's programing.

On Jan. 31, 2000, a letter to "Dear KCPT" was received in an envelope that bore the stamp of the Kansas Department of Corrections, Lansing, Kan. The letter concerned the series "Portrait of a Family" which the writer called "a very educational series and a compliment to your already exceptional programming." The correspondence continued:

I would like to propose that you please consider a "barter." Will explain.

I would like to receive a videotape copy of this series. In return I will give KCPT and its viewers a hand carved leather picture of an American Bald Eagle framed to be used for auction on KCPT to help pay for the programming of such fine shows as you broadcast.

My need for a copy of "Portrait of a Family" is for use in one of the treatment programs here at the Lansing Correctional Facility.

The leather carving I offer for barter is 14 x 12, framed and very fine quality work. The last one that I made sold for $165.00.

If for any reason this is not acceptable please inform me of the cost for a copy of this series and I will raise the funds.

American people don't believe anything until they see it on television.

– RICHARD NIXON,
37th president of the United States

Reed responded with detailed information about the source of the videotape and how it might be obtained.

As part of the city's sesquicentennial celebrations, Jeannette and Miller Nichols conceived and funded a five-part series, "Uniquely Kansas City: A History of the Arts." It chronicled the city's transformation from cowtown to Midwestern cultural mecca. The high-definition television broadcast premiered to high praise May 2000 in an AMC theater, again courtesy of Marjorie Grant.

The showing made KCPT the first television station in the Kansas City market to create, produce and broadcast a feature-length HDTV documentary. *The Star's* Barnhart noted how brilliantly high definition captured night scenes — snowflakes passing through the Community Christian Church's "steeple of light" and the "proud, serene visage" of Charlie Parker on the Bird's statue near 18th and Vine. Part one of the series, "The Art of Making a City Beautiful," received the 2001 Preservation Award from the Historic Kansas City Foundation and would also win a media award from NETA.

The framework for the KCPT-produced documentary "Over Here: The Story of Kansas City & World War II" was the recollections of that war by 30 local residents. In July, "Conversations with Cynthia Smith" premiered with a chat with Kansas First Lady Linda Graves, an episode that concluded with a memorable Gusewelle video essay on succumbing to the attraction of a LaMar's doughnut.

PHOTOGRAPH BY CHRISTOPHER HIRSHEIMER, LIDIA'S ITALY IN AMERICA, ALFRED A. KNOPF, ©2011.

Lidia Bastianich not only had a full lineup of shows on PBS, she owned a popular Kansas City restaurant.

MOKAN'S REACH: 350,000 STUDENTS

By this time, the MoKan Kids Network was a highly successful partnership of KCPT, Smoky Hills Public Television (Kansas), and 250 school districts across Kansas and Missouri impacting 350,000 students and 30,000 teachers. At a Washington, D.C., meeting, the Association of America's Public Television Stations (APTS) awarded KCPT its 21st Century Award for extraordinary leadership and innovation in developing the network.

The MoKan name was changed when Carbondale, Illinois' WSIU-TV was added to the network. It became the "ChalkWaves" channel. ChalkWaves competed successfully with for-profit video suppliers because it was server-based and did not overload schools' narrow connection to the Internet.

The documentary "Lidia's Kansas City" told the story of the first restaurant venture outside New York City of Lidia Bastianich, Italy's answer to Julia Child. She was already established as a fixture in PBS's lineup of cooking shows, with "Lidia's Italian-American Kitchen," then "Lidia's Family Table" and "Lidia's Italy,"

For the loot, honey, for the loot.

— AVA GARDNER,

on her reason for coming out of retirement to appear in a soap opera

Appraisers from the "Antiques Roadshow" made well-attended stops in Kansas City.

Louis Ruiz received national recognition for his work with KCPT's Community Advisory Board.

KCPT partnered with *The Kansas City Star*, KMBC-TV and KCUR radio in a live broadcast of a debate among the Democratic gubernatorial candidates.

"Salute to Heroes" was a tribute to World War II combat veteran and former U.S. Sen. Bob Dole at the July opening of the Robert J. Dole Institute of Politics at the University of Kansas. Taped by KCPT at the Lied Center in Lawrence, the two-hour program was hosted by Tom Brokaw and featured former Presidents Gerald R. Ford and Jimmy Carter. It was aired as a "Screen Time" special on Channel 19.

"And Thou Shalt Honor: a Town Hall Program on Health Care," aired in September. It was a 90-minute discussion among Kansas City health care leaders moderated by Nick Haines.

In October 2003, the popular PBS Antiques Roadshow, with its free appraisals of antiques and collectibles, made Kansas City stops on three consecutive Mondays. And there was another enjoyable trip with the Gusewelles, this time to Spain, netting $8,000 again.

That same month, Carolyn Watley, CBIZ Benefits & Insurance executive, succeeded Jim Duncan as PT 19 chair. An article in *Kansas City Hispanic News* about board member Louis Ruiz noted that as second vice president of the national organization Friends of Public Television, Ruiz was involved in Washington lobbying efforts for continued funding of public television. He had been honored by APTS in 1998 at a ceremony in Washington, D.C., for his work with KCPT's Community Advisory Board.

'BE GOOD SMILE PRETTY'

On Nov. 11, 2003, "Be Good Smile Pretty" made its debut on the PBS "Independent Lens" program. The KCPT documentary was about a girl who never knew her father, Navy Lt. Donald G. Droz, from Rich Hill, Mo. All she had were stories and a few pictures of him holding her when she was three months old. He was killed in Vietnam shortly after the pictures were taken, when his patrol boat was ambushed on his first day back from that brief vacation with the little girl and her mother. The film was a tremendous success, winning a $25,000 cash prize at the Los Angeles Film Festival.

"Be Good Smile Pretty" was nominated for the National Academy of Television Arts and Sciences' 2003 Documentary Emmy. The nomination was a great tribute, and co-producers Randy Mason and Michael Murphy were invited to New York for the award ceremony, the 25th Annual News & Documentary Emmy

(Continued on page 133)

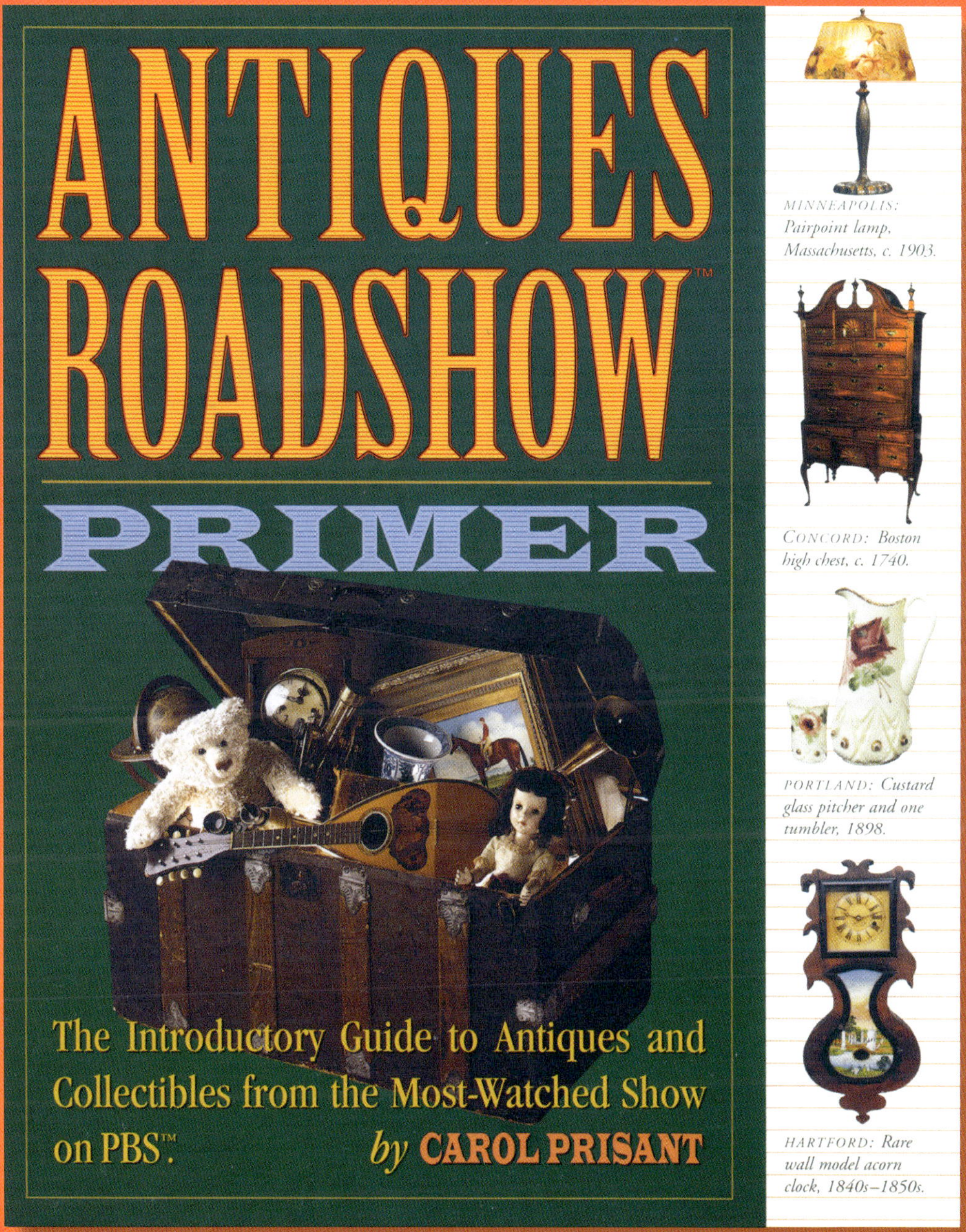

The addictive "Antiques Roadshow" got its start in the U.K. in 1977 and premiered across the pond in 1997. Few guests got rich, but that hasn't stopped many of us from taking just one more look through grandpa's stamp collection.

JILL TOYOSHIBA/THE KANSAS CITY STAR

As part of a film about her father, a kneeling Tracy Droz Tragos watched as engraver Jesse Schowengerdt prepared to add the words "Husband" and "Father" to her father's tombstone in Rich Hill, Mo. Also watching, from top left, were sister-in-law and cameraperson Kat Tragos, mother Judith Droz Keyes and grandmother Dorothy Droz. Top, Navy Lt. Don Droz, who was killed in Vietnam when Tracy was three months old.

Yes, it's the actual Emmy.

"Be Good, Smile Pretty" is featured on the cover of KCPT Magazine.

(Continued from page 130)
Awards. Droz's daughter, Tracy Droz Tragos, the film's producer and writer was there to make the speech, should luck prevail. The little girl of the story was now a grown woman, with children of her own.

Tragos, a San Francisco resident, had conceived of the documentary and sent an introductory trailer to KCPT. There, Mason and Murphy recognized a great story and helped with the production. Tragos formed a charitable organization, the Orphans of War Foundation, to champion the project and to help raise funds for the production. (She was one of more than 20,000 children who lost a father in the Vietnam War.)

The Emmy ceremony promised to be a great show, attended by a host of television luminaries and lesser lights. (Murphy said he suspected that the "Be Good" trio was invited to fill out the hall.) Once on the scene, they found the large Marriott Marquis Hotel auditorium filled with better known honorees and major network personalities and took their assigned seats anonymously in the back of the room. The program was hosted by Peter Jennings. Dan Rather presented the Emmys, and Tom Brokaw was honored with a lifetime achievement award. The recently retired Bill Moyers was in the audience and was recognized with a standing ovation.

The national Emmy for best documentary was the grand finale, and in the course of the long evening, the KCPT delegation had made itself comfortable — Tragos kicked off her shoes. The winners of various categories were big budget productions from major producers.

When the climactic moment arrived, KCPT's "Be Good Smile Pretty" was named the best documentary of 2003. Among those surprised were Tragos, Mason and Murphy. Tragos located her shoes, and the unlikely champions made their way to the front of the room. It was a long trek, so time-consuming that the introductory music ended long before they reached the stage to accept their Emmy from Rather.

The trophy now resides in its own glass case in the KCPT lobby — a reminder of what arguably was KCPT's finest hour, Kansas City's only national Emmy. The engraving reads:

2003 News and Documentary Awards
Best Documentary
"Be Good Smile Pretty"
PBS
KCPT

Board member Hunter Wolbach initiated a campaign to interest a new generation of young professionals in supporting KCPT, which culminated in the election of two of them to the PT 19 board.

In November, KCPT received this letter:

Dear Station Manager,

The enclosed letter was written by our five-year-old kindergarten son, who is the world's #1 Thomas the Tank Engine fan.

He was delighted beyond expression that Thomas was being broadcast this fall on Saturdays at 7:00 a.m. He was very disappointed when the programming changed to Sunday mornings at 8:30 a.m. We encouraged him to write a letter expressing his opinion and circulate a petition to assess the feelings of his peers. The petition is also enclosed.

We are a cable-free household and watch very little television. The television we do let our son watch is 100% KCPT programming.

Thank you for having such family-oriented, value-filled programming.

Sincerely,

Enclosed was this crayon-printed letter, decorated with a sketch of Thomas.

Dear KCPT: Can you change Thomas to Saturdays? At 7:00 A.M.!

One of yours, Coleman

There also was the "petition" — a separate page headed "We ager (agree)," with eleven printed names.

In response, Bill Reed invited Coleman to tour KCPT.

Recently, Coleman Brockmeir, now 13, wrote another letter:

I was 5 when I wrote a letter to KCPT because they had moved "Thomas the Tank Engine" to Sunday morning from Saturday morning. This caused a scheduling conflict, as we regularly attended church on Sundays. I dearly loved Thomas and this new time came just short of causing an earthquake in my home.

To help vent my frustrations, my mom suggested that I write a letter and a petition to KCPT to try to get them to change the show's time. I went to my church and to my school, collecting tons of signatures.

Soon after I mailed my appeal in, I received a letter from the station manager inviting me to come and visit KCPT on a private tour. I was overjoyed! I was allowed to bring along a friend and I chose Harrison Boldt. The two of us were treated to learning how the station worked and how shows are shot. We got a t-shirt and got to see ourselves in the camera. It was a blast.

Thomas still wasn't moved back to the time I wanted. I taped the shows, but it just wasn't the same. Recently I was watching KCPT and noticed that Thomas has again been scheduled to Saturday morning!

That year the KCPT float won first place in the Media Division of the St. Patrick's Day parade.

(Continued on page 138)

Thomas the Tank Engine is a fictional steam locomotive that started life in the British Railway Series of books by the Rev. Wilbert Awdry.

Channel 19 President Bill Reed hosts Coleman Brockmeir, left, and Harrison Boldt at KCPT.

Coleman and Harrison get a tutorial on what it takes to get a show on the air.

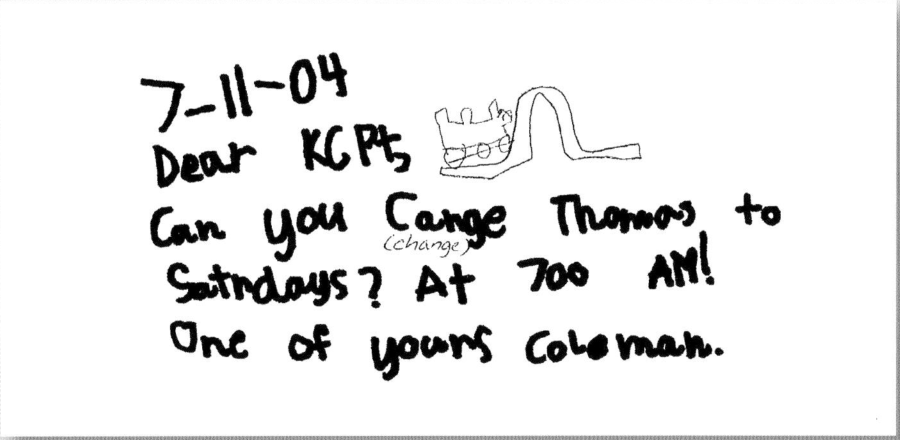

7-11-04
Dear KCPt,
Can you Cange (change) Thomas to
Satrdays? At 700 AM!
One of yours Coleman.

we — ager (Agree)

Coleman
Kim Hoeven
Todd Blade
JACK
Robert MATT
NICKO
Harrison
GARRETT
ISAAC
To MATTHEW

Cynthia Smith left Channel 19 to become president and CEO of the children's shelter Sunflower House.

Victor Hogstrom became KCPT president and CEO in 2005.

(Continued from page 136)

One of the casualties of the 2002 belt-tightening was "Ruckus." There was some applause at the demise — one viewer sent a check for $100 in appreciation. Another wrote that he had complained several times about "the right-wing slant of programming, particularly 'Ruckus,' " and expressed approval of the cancellation. To disappointed "Ruckus" supporters, Reed explained that the cancellation was a result of budget problems that necessitated staff reductions by 26 positions and elimination of two other local programs before making the "painful decision" to cancel "Ruckus." But one viewer believed that the cancellation was not for financial reasons but was a form of censorship of ideas and opinions not supported by the station.

After a two-year interruption, "Ruckus" resumed with a new set, new faces and a new perspective. Mike Shanin, moderator of the program since 1995, was now also the managing editor. At an April 2005 PT 19 Board meeting, Cynthia Smith reported that ratings were up, the fan club was growing and the program had increased its viewer numbers from 9,512 to 20,573.

On June 26, Bill Reed made a memorable appearance on Jim Lehrer's NewsHour, offering a spirited, articulate defense of PBS. His words provoked an avalanche of correspondence. They also generated financial support for KCPT, including $1,000 from a Kansas City viewer, a $100 check from Cupertino, Calif., and the following from the Sisters of Charity of Leavenworth:

> *We always renew our membership in the Fall but last night after listening to you on the Lehrer Newshour we all decided that we must send you a bit of appreciation in the form of this small check.*

In July, Reed lamented the departure of Cynthia Smith to become president and CEO of the child-protection center Sunflower House. Reed retired July 31, 2005, after 13 highly productive years at KCPT. Board members were invited to a VIP retirement party "to celebrate a long and wonderful career." Reed later was inducted into the Silver Circle of the National Television Academy, which honored him for his "significant contribution to the television industry."

A CEO FROM CHATTANOOGA

Victor Hogstrom, formerly president of WTCI-TV 45 in Chattanooga, Tenn., became the new president and CEO of KCPT, which now had an annual operating budget of $7 million.

The British film industry is not dead —
it's alive and well and it's called television.
– LORD GUS MacDONALD,
Scottish journalist, media executive, member of the House of Lords,
and Glasgow Caledonian University chancellor

In his first year, Hogstrom added two new locally-produced weekly programs, "Talk Back Live With Steve Rose," the veteran Johnson County, Kan., newspaper publisher and one-time "Ruckus" panelist, and "One on One with Victor Hogstrom," a program of interviews with local persons of interest, such as jazz legend Marilyn Maye and Chiefs head coach Herm Edwards. Hogstrom also was a fan of British comedies: He increased the number presented and formed a "BritCom Club" of enthusiasts willing to offer financial support. He also campaigned for a digital mobile studio to cover special events and implemented enhanced underwriting spots that allowed underwriters to do more than merely utter company names. (The FCC now permitted this, but Bill Reed had not been a fan — in his view it smacked too much of advertising — and KCPT was among the last public TV stations in the country to make the switch.)

Steve McDowell followed Joanne Collins as PT 19 chair.

In October 2005, Steve McDowell succeeded Joanne Collins in the PT 19 chair.

In 2006, Congress advanced the move to digital TV by prohibiting analog broadcasts after February 2009. KCPT placed a new digital transmitter in service in January 2006, funded by a 2005 CPB grant, with the Hall Family Foundation and KCPT contributing matching dollars. The result was a dramatic improvement to the broadcast signal; the station was now well positioned for the digital future.

Saxophonist Bobby Watson was part of a "Screen Time" 90th birthday tribute concert to Josephine Baker.

In February 2006, KCPT's "Screen Time" program presented "Jazz at the Gem; a Tribute to Josephine Baker." It was a 90th birthday tribute, with a special all-star concert at Kansas City's Gem Theatre, hosted by actress Leslie Uggams and featuring the 18th and Vine Jazz Band fronted by Kansas City's legendary saxophonist Bobby Watson.

In June 2006, KCPT aired an hour-long documentary on Kansas City's most famous land developer, J.C. Nichols: "Community Builder: The Life and Legacy of J.C. Nichols." It also formed a partnership with Children's Mercy Hospital to provide workshops for parents and hospital staff in early-childhood brain development. And the Francis Family Foundation and the Junior League continued their financial support of KCPT Reads, the station's early literacy initiative.

On June 20, Channel 19 broadcast "Stories Under the Stone," a one-hour Charles Gusewelle documentary produced by KCPT and funded by the Courtney S. Turner Trust. As Gusewelle wrote:

> *The grave is the most democratic of destinations. It's the station to which all journeyers are finally bound — tycoons and political bosses, city boosters and builders, working folk, adventurers, the lucky and luckless alike. And each of them has a story.*

A "Rare Visions & Roadside Revelations" art find made a striking KCPT Magazine *cover.*

Larry Hawks became PT 19 chairman at the October 2006 annual meeting. Carol Marinovitch, the former mayor of the Unified Government of Wyandotte County/Kansas City, Kan., was elected to the board. She would be a very effective chair for the board's legislative affairs committee.

The ability to respond favorably to viewer programming requests was often out of the station's control. Financial strictures or availability came into play. One viewer wrote:

> *I depend on Channel 19 to help me keep my sanity in a difficult world! I used to watch Classical Stretch & Priscilla's Yoga at 6 in the morning, but now it's gone. ... Charlie Rose & Tavis Smiley are also my favorites but do you have to show them soooo late at night?*

Hogstrom had to respond that the yoga program was too expensive without a sponsor, and the Rose and Smiley programs were late night satellite offerings geared to a more mature audience.

In 2007, KCPT Kids had a new mascot. PT (pronounced "Petey"), a baby owl, was the offspring of a partnership between KCPT (Angee Simmons) and Bazillion Pictures, a Kansas City animation firm, and was funded by a grant from the H&R Block Foundation. It was part of a campaign to send new literacy messages to kids throughout the daytime period.

IS THERE NO END TO THE FAN CLUB?

On Jan. 4, 2007, "Rare Visions and Roadside Revelations" began its 11th season with 13 new shows. There was no budget for marketing the series — viewers around the country just stumbled across it.

> *I saw your program on PBS ... I don't know how I missed it in the past, but I plan on watching it from now on. I went on line and checked out your web site. I found several places I plan on visiting with my family. Thank you for such a great show that you all share with us.*

> *Hi guys. Just saw one of your programs for the first time today on the PBS station and I am in tee total love with you all and your show!!!! WOO HOO! I want to get your whole DVD collection but I just wanted to thank you for producing such a wonderful show and I hope to see many, many of them.*

(Continued on page 143)

The "world's largest ball of twine" was made in Cawker City, Kan., in the '50s by Frank Stoeber — who was tired of all those loose strands getting in the way. In the '80s, when other towns started competing with their big balls of twine, Cawker City started an annual Twine-a-Thon and built another ball (behind the Weasels) to make sure that the record stayed at home.

Above, Sam "The Dot Man" McMillan, from Winston-Salem, N.C., painted the bench in the collage on page 96. Top, at the Museum of Mirth, Mystery and Mayhem in St. Louis you can see the world's largest pair of underwear and the honeymoon trailer that Elvis and Priscilla Presley once shared. The Weasels found it all on the 3rd floor of the City Museum.

(Continued from page 140)

Countless other emails were proof of continuing popularity. A representative few:

> *Your show is one of my all-time favorites. My mother and I watch it every Sunday in Burgaw, Pender County, North Carolina. (That's Hurricane Alley to you guys.) Please make more shows. We love them!*

> *Just wondering if you all were on the road still? I noticed you haven't posted any new trips. I love the show but haven't seen any episodes on KETC (St. Louis) lately. I'm getting ready to take a trip in June for about 4 weeks and may stop in on a few places.*

> *Your show is awesome! Keep driving! I saw an episode the other day that had you at a park like place where someone used wood for walking bridges and outdoor landscape art. I could have sworn, as I caught the tail end, that you said you went "back across the border" into Arkansas to finish. Any idea what I am looking for?*

> *I love your show. I watch it as faithfully as I can. I am a folk artist also, and I totally appreciate your discovery of other folk artists.*

> *We love the souvenirs you get during your travels, but we would like to experience them up close and personal! Are you hogging them to yourselves or is there some kind of "museum" of those things of wonder and joy?*

> *I just returned from Portland, Ore., where I saw the Velveteria. The folks there didn't know they had been on RVRR. They remembered Randy Mason and claimed Don the Camera Guy did great impressions of Richard Nixon and others ... Their collection is growing, as is their collection of the black velvet arts. Glad I remembered seeing the place featured on your always tasteful, if not downright informative, program.*

Gary Warmack created his mixed media "Pharaoh" after being shot and, in a near death state, felt himself whisked across time and space, cultures and civilizations. The Weasels found Warmack in Bethlehem, Pa., where he translates his experience into art.

57 Channels (And Nothin' On)
– BRUCE SPRINGSTEEN
song from his album "Human Touch," 1992

Simmons, left, was nine month's pregnant when the battle scenes were shot.

"Bad Blood" was more like a motion picture than a documentary, James said. "We had horses, wagons, firearms, cannons, actors, extras, craft services, makeup, a 100-foot green screen for the burning of Lawrence and, of course, period costumes."

Simmons was nine months pregnant when the battle scenes were shot and sure that she was going into labor during the canon fire:

> *It started out as let's do a documentary about the border war and it turned into a two-year feature film with nearly 200 extras and re-enactors when it was all said and done. The largest production to date. We had no idea what we were getting into when we started. The costs for something like this would typically be astronomical, so we solicited family members to help.*
>
> *My husband grew a classic 1850s beard so he could play the role of John Brown's son. I had my mom baking cookies out of my kitchen and making spaghetti for 50 hungry bushwackers so we wouldn't have to pay for catering, and my father-in-law brought out his 1980 mini-Wini to serve as our makeup and dressing room. We even solicited our dog to be in a couple of shots.*

(Continued on page 148)

The "documentary" turned into a feature film with 200 extras.

The y
a final gi
Garden a
At th
PT 19 cha
In No
on Chann
raised by
ceremoni
January 2
donated b
"As Time C
of Dibley."
The K
School Di
Novembe
students.
to suppor
in school

At the end o
of roadside

The official poster of the 90-minute film.

KEITH MYERS/THE KANSAS CITY STAR

Above, Fed chairman Ben Bernanke, left, greets the former chairman of the Denver branch, Thomas Williams, in KC's new Federal Reserve Bank building. Left, Helzberg Hall in the new Center for the Performing Arts. Top, "Generation XL." Right, "Meet the Past."

08

2008 After months of unraveling, the economy finally crashes. The investment bank Lehman Brothers files for bankruptcy and President Bush puts mortgage giants Fannie Mae and Freddie Mac under government conservatorship.

2008 Barack Obama is elected President with 52.8 percent of the vote.

2009 With 20 cases confirmed, the swine flu outbreak is declared a public health emergency.

2009 Musician, pop singer and superstar Michael Jackson dies at age 50.

2009 Senator Edward Kennedy, who has served in the Senate for 46 years, dies of brain cancer at the age of 77.

A STATION TO WATCH

2008–2011

CHANNEL 19 SEEMED TO HAVE RAISED ITS GAME — AGAIN. AS THE FINANCIAL CRISIS GATHERED STEAM, IT TAPED FEDERAL RESETRVE CHAIRMAN BEN BERNANKE AND "NEWSHOUR'S" JIM LEHRER DISSECTING THE ECONOMY AT A TOWN HALL MEETING AT THE KANSAS CITY FEDERAL RESERVE BUILDING. IN THREE YEARS, LOCALLY GROWN PRODUCTIONS EXPLORED WHY YOUNG PEOPLE HERE WEIGH TOO MUCH (IN THREE PARTS); HOW THE MUCH-LAUDED ACOUSTICS AT HELZBERG HALL REALLY SOUND; AND HOW A CONVERSATION WITH BOSS TOM PENDERGAST MIGHT HAVE GONE. *KANSAS CITY STAR* TV CRITIC AARON BARNHART RECENTLY CALLED KCPT "THE KANSAS CITY PUBLIC TV STATION THAT CONTINUES TO OUTPERFORM ITS 31ST-LARGEST-MARKET STATURE." THE VIEWERS WILL DECIDE. THE BOOK ENDS, BUT THE STORY GOES ON.

2009 The documentary style comedy "Modern Family" premieres to critical acclaim, including that of the First Family: President Obama says it's his favorite show to watch with his family. The action occurs in three interrelated households and capitalizes on the idea that the modern family is a unit that is always taking its own psychological temperature.

2010 An explosion and fire on the Deepwater Horizon oil rig in the Gulf of Mexico kills 11 and sets in motion a personal, economic and ecological tragedy the extent of which may never be tallied.

2010 The U.S. Senate votes 65-31 to end the ban against openly gay men and women serving in the military.

2011 Judging from its popularity, the British-American series "Downtown Abbey" — about the Crawley family and their servants in the years before World War I —has relevance today.

11

Well, gentlemen, you have now invented the biggest time-waster of all time. Use it well.

— SIR ISAAC SHOENBERG,
British electronics engineer, following his team's 1932 demonstration of the Emitron electronic television camera tube

Channel 19 produced a 2008 documentary on Kansas City philanthropist and builder R.A. Long, who died in 1934.

Simmons picks up a regional Emmy for her documentary "Assembly Required."

"Generation XL" was a 2008 three-part series on obesity in young people hosted by Nick Haines.

In 2008, the R.A. Long Historical Society produced a Channel 19 documentary about the Kansas City lumber baron and philanthropist who died in 1934 and was the driving force behind construction of Liberty Memorial. Long also built Longview Farm in Lee's Summit in 1914. He famously employed 50 Belgian craftsmen and 200 Sicilian stonemasons among the 2,000 workers who took 18 months to turn 1,780 raw acres into "the world's most beautiful farm."

An Angee Simmons documentary team photographed high school students from Shawnee Mission North, Raytown South and Liberty as they designed and built robots for the Robotics Challenge, a program of FIRST Robotics (For Inspiration and Recognition of Science and Technology). The resulting documentary, "Assembly Required," was telecast Feb. 28, 2008, on Channel 19. It would receive a regional Emmy and resulted in Simmons becoming an advocate for science and engineering education in schools.

EXTRA LARGE AND GROWING

Also in February, Nick Haines hosted the first installment of a new series, "Generation XL." It was a series of programs concerned with obesity in young people, primarily funded by health insurer Blue Cross/Blue Shield with an assist from the Health Care Foundation of Greater Kansas City. The initial production, "The Rise and Fall of Physical Education," was praised by parents, educators and concerned residents throughout the Kansas City metropolitan area. It was followed by "The Food Fight in the School Cafeteria" and then "The Battle over School Vending Machines."

Episodes continue and have inspired positive responses — motivating parents to join the PTA, gym class instructors to take action and teachers to discontinue rewarding classroom performance with high calorie treats. The series received two National Educational Telecommunications Association awards, and a DVD set of the series was mailed to 1,200 principals, superintendents and school board members.

In March, the new show "Meet the Past" with Crosby Kemper III introduced a series of interviews with famous local figures, beginning with political boss Tom Pendergast. Pendergast was portrayed, re-enactor style, by University of Missouri-Kansas City Professor William Worley as Kemper engaged him in conversation. A good start to the series, the interview received a regional Emmy nomination. Kemper was the enterprising chief executive who had transformed the Kansas City Public Library System, and KCPT filmed the interviews in the imposing Grand

(Continued on page 155)

KCPT producer Angee Simmons and videographers Don Mayberger and Dave Burkhardt followed three area high school robotics teams in a national competition to design and build a robot. Pictured, the Liberty High School Robotics team and the fruits of their labors.

The first episode in the popular "Meet the Past" series paired host and Kansas City Public Library CEO Crosby Kemper III with University of Missouri-Kansas City Professor William Worley as Tom Pendergast.

(Continued from page 152)
Hall of the Central Library. The program's creator, Henry Fortunato, was the library's director of public affairs. KCPT members were invited to be part of the audience, and they turned out in large numbers for the telecasts.

A costumed version of PT, the book-loving owl, made his debut at the KC Literacy Festival on the Country Club Plaza. He also passed out the first edition of *KCPT Kids News* at the May board meeting.

Nick Haines was honored by Johnson County Community College, the Missouri Association of Social Welfare and The Pitch.

OFF THE AIR WITH HIM!

On May 1, Nick Haines received the "Headline Award" from the Johnson County Community College's department of journalism and media communications at a luncheon at the college. In 2006, he had been named by *The Pitch* weekly as Kansas City's best TV host and also was honored by the Missouri Association of Social Welfare with its annual Excellence in Journalism Award. His distinctive British inflections were an asset, although Haines recalls one irate caller demanding that KCPT "get that guy with the fake British accent off the air."

Jim Lehrer visited the KCPT studio on May 15 and lunched on May 16 with leaders of the Kansas City Chamber of Commerce and the Civic Council.

The unique relationship with commercial stations continued. On May 22, Channel 19 telecast "Kansas City's Most Wanted," produced by KCPT's Sean Holmes with the aid of a $10,000 grant from the Kansas City Crime Commission. In his column about the program in *The Kansas City Star,* Aaron Barnhart wrote:

> *In recent years, KCPT has become the de facto leader in local public affairs programming — because the other stations gave up on public affairs to do more news. Journalists on other stations appear on Nick Haines' "Week in Review" show. In a way, KCPT is giving back, not just to Kansas City, but to those stations that lend their talents to Haines every week.*

Producer Sean Holmes won awards for "Kansas City's Most Wanted," conceived by the Kansas City Crime Commission.

"Kansas City's Most Wanted" was conceived by the Crime Commission president, Rick Easley, in the hope that it might help bring some of the area's more notorious fugitives to justice.

A new four-part sequel to 2000's "Uniquely Kansas City" was produced in May 2008, hosted by Randy Mason and Steph Suetos and funded by the Miller and Jeannette Nichols Charitable Foundation, the Hartwigs and the J.B. Reynolds Foundation. The co-producer, with Mason, was Sandy Woodson. In addition to serving as writer/producer, Woodson is an archivist and harbors much of the institutional memory of KCPT. She is currently employed as the receptionist. The new series showcased the city's current music, theater, dance and visual arts for each of the four seasons of the year. Woodson interviewed more than 100 local artists for the production.

Memorial Day weekend brought a rousing televised performance, "Celebration at the Station" with the Kansas City Symphony, destined to become an annual outdoor patriotic celebration rivaling the Fourth of July PBS production on the National Mall.

Randy Mason, pictured, and Sandy Woodson produced a sequel to "Uniquely Kansas City."

KCPT produced "10-J: The History of the Federal Reserve Bank of Kansas City," a documentary narrated by Susie Gharib of the PBS "Nightly Business Report." The telecast was previewed in the Truman Forum of the Plaza Branch Library and aired in June, the month the Fed's impressive new home in midtown Kansas City was completed.

Pam James interviewed the people of the Fed's vast Tenth District (the system's second largest) for the program, traveling from Oklahoma City and Denver to the heart of Missouri. There was exclusive access to the Bureau of Engraving and Printing in Fort Worth, Texas; the Denver Mint; and the original Federal Reserve documents in the National Archives in Washington, D.C. The documentary won a first place award in the Special Programs category from the Missouri Broadcasters Association.

PBS "Nightly Business Report" anchor Susie Gharib narrated a KCPT documentary on the Federal Reserve Bank.

HEARD ANYTHING ABOUT THE NEW DELI?

In the absence of actual statistics, casual observation would indicate that Kansas City is an "eating out" town. "Check Please," a review of local restaurants, had a successful debut. Moderator Doug Frost, one of only three people in the world who is both a master sommelier and master of wine, is the knowledgeable host, joined by guests who critique their dining experiences at the featured eateries.

The format is simple and suspenseful. Each episode has three guests; each recommends his or her favorite restaurant. The other two guests go and experience that restaurant for themselves, then they all meet back at the KCPT studio and opinions fly. The reviewers are from all walks of life (they share only a passion for food) and from all over the metro area. The establishments visited are not limited to high-end places, but include bistros, cafes, greasy spoons and dives. Bank of America and board member Lafayette Ford were the initial funders.

KCPT's restaurant review show is a favorite in a foody town.

There was an encouraging capital campaign report detailing grants from the Hall Family Foundation, the Gottlieb Foundation, various Kemper funds at United Missouri Bank and the Muriel McBride Kauffman Foundation.

In July 2008, Victor Hogstrom stepped down as KCPT president and CEO to pursue other interests. Chairman Jay Meschke commented that Hogstrom had been instrumental in helping place the station on firm financial ground, as well as a talented broadcasting executive. Hogstrom was succeeded on an interim basis by Susan Stanton, who had most recently been president and CEO of United Way

(Continued on page 158)

MIKE RANSDELL/THE KANSAS CITY STAR

Channel 19 televised "Celebration at the Station," the Memorial Day extravaganza with the Kansas City Symphony.

This instrument can teach, it can illuminate, yes, it can even inspire. But it can do so only to the extent that humans are determined to use it to those ends. Otherwise, it is merely lights and wires in a box.

— EDWARD R. MURROW,

American broadcast journalist of unparalleled influence ("This....is London")

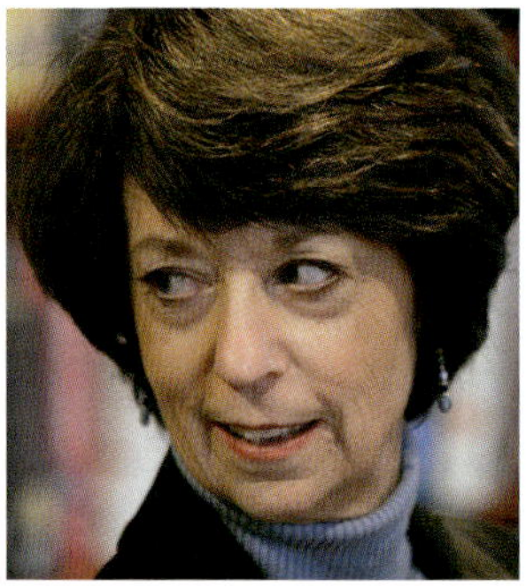

Susan Stanton became interim KCPT president and CEO.

(Continued from page 156)

of Greater Kansas City. Before that, she was president of Payless Cashways and held executive positions with H&R Block and the Ewing Marion Kauffman Foundation.

The Channel 19 auction had outlived its usefulness and was canceled. Only a few PBS stations still conduct these fundraisers, and PBS has closed its auction support department. Auction interruptions of regularly scheduled programming continued to be a problem with KCPT viewers, and proceeds were no longer significant to the bottom line. However, the auction was the catalyst for early community involvement in KCPT by enthusiastic volunteers and cooperative commercial stations, and its role in the visibility and development of the station was crucial.

Jeff Evans, KCPT vice president for technology and broadcasting, is one who recalls the excitement of the broadcasts and even enjoyed the long on-air hours required of the engineering crew. Auctions sometimes continued well past midnight, with volunteers by the hundreds on hand to operate phone banks, serve as auctioneers and share the experience.

Jim Lehrer and the "NewsHour" carried gavel-to-gavel coverage of the Democratic National Convention in August, broadcast on KCPT; the Republican National Convention in September received the same treatment.

The scheduled seventh annual black tie dinner party on the Liberty Memorial deck was washed out. In the future, there would be a contingency plan to allow for Mother Nature's caprices.

On Sept. 16, KCPT supporter and Kansas City Kansan columnist Rudy Padilla wrote Jay Meschke expressing concern over "the lack of inclusion of Hispanic Americans in PBS programming." He and Jesse Gonzales spoke on the subject to the PT 19 board at its September meeting. Padilla was state commander of the American GI Forum, a Hispanic veteran's organization, and it was in that capacity that he addressed the board. He would continue to press for more Hispanic recognition.

On Oct. 10, U.S. Rep. Sam Graves turned down a "Kansas City Week in Review" debate with his opponent in a Missouri Congressional race, former Kansas City Mayor Kay Barnes. As a result, there was an empty chair on the set during Barnes' 10-minute interview with host Nick Haines. (Graves won the election.) Two days later, there was an hour-long debate on Channel 19 between two Kansas congressional candidates, U.S. Rep. Dennis Moore and state Sen. Nick Jordan.

On Oct. 11, the Mid-America Regional Council hosted the televised initial session of "Imagine KC" before a large MARC headquarters audience and at four remote sites. Community members in attendance had come together to talk about the manner in which the region built structures, provided transportation and infrastructure and consumed resources. It was a prelude to envisioning an improved future for the metro area. "Imagine KC" was a partnership of KCPT with MARC, the University of Kansas and others, funded by the Federal Highway Administration.

After a series of workshops, the project culminated in April 2009 with Channel 19 engaging about 80,000 residents sharing their vision of a region more vibrant, connected and green. This spawned several derivative "Imagine KC" productions, co-produced with MARC and broadcast on KCPT.

At the annual meeting on Oct. 14, Hallmark's Tracy McFerrin-Foster succeeded Jay Meschke as Channel 19 chair.

In October, KCPT received a grant from the Hartwigs to renew "Rare Visions and Roadside Revelations." An Oct. 16 Barnhart column began:

> *The 12th season of "Rare Visions and Roadside Revelations" begins tonight on KCPT, and once again the tireless hunters of folk-art treasures are going where they have never gone before.*
>
> *To high definition TV.*
>
> *And to Nevada.*
>
> *In 11 previous seasons the "Rare Visions" minivan had managed to visit every other state in the lower 48 west of the Hudson. Somehow, though, their relentless pursuit of the oddball never took them even near Las Vegas.*

The column went on to recite some of the highlights to be anticipated, including the "jaw-dropping home and memorabilia" museum of a former Nevada lieutenant governor who was a neurosurgeon and played in a band called the Dummkopfs, and Eliphante, a three-acre compound near Sedona, Ariz., built by hippies.

Barnhart also noted that viewers would get to see everything "in super-sharp high definition for the first time." He reported that Randy Mason continued to hear from far-flung fans of the show, and quoted him:

> *I'm from a small town. It's important that when someone is a little different, you not make fun of them, even if they're a little goofy. If that comes through, I'm happy.*

"Kids on Ice" was scheduled for Kansas City's Crown Center Ice Terrace. The PT board was told in November that Citibank, one of the sponsors of the popular event, had just laid off 53,000 employees but would honor its "Kids on Ice" commitment. Gamma Phi Beta was another sponsor, and Starbucks provided coffee and hot chocolate. *(Continued on page 161)*

American GI Forum commander Rudy Padilla advocated for more latino representation in KCPT programming.

IMAGINE KC

The community came together to talk building and infrastructure in "Imagine KC."

Top, "Imagine KC" filming live in the studio. Above, producing the show in a studio control room.

(Continued from page 159)

Kliff Kuehl became KCPT's president and CEO in April 2009, following Susan Stanton.

The new CEO had been managing KNPB-TV in Reno, Nev., a station serving northern Nevada and northeastern California. KNPB's board chair praised the departing Kuehl's accomplishments, citing in particular expansion into new media such as timely, low-cost audio news reports. Kuehl also had increased local production, public affairs programming and community outreach activities.

Upon arrival at his new job, he commended Stanton and the PT 19 board for making tough economic calls, shedding full-time employees and ending Channel 19's long-running auction. He noted that many stations were still "doing furloughs and cuts" but there were no plans for this at Channel 19. His goal for KCPT: "to make the greatest possible impact we possibly can on our community."

Kliff Kuehl came from Reno, Nev., to become president and CEO of KCPT.

KC Studio made its debut with the May-June 2009 edition. The bi-monthly magazine combines the KCPT member magazine with a comprehensive arts guide, the result of a collaboration of KCPT with the dazzling new Kauffman Center for the Performing Arts and Townsend Publications. The Kauffman Foundation financed the expanded publication.

The new bi-monthly KC Studio had a comprehensive arts guide.

Minutes of a May 27, 2009, PT board meeting reported the following:

> *Tracy Foster welcomed our visitor, Renee Walker. Bonnie Rabicoff reported that we have received a bequest from Mrs. Walker's late husband, Ron.*
>
> *Walker spoke of how meaningful KCPT was in her husband's life. She was a first grade teacher and encouraged her husband to have his reading, language and spelling skills evaluated. It came as a relief to know there was a reason for a lifelong problem — dyslexia.*
>
> *Ron was interested in many aspects of life — curious, creative and inventive. He watched public television consistently, and had a great deal of trust in KCPT. He found the programming interesting, intelligent, true and thoughtful — books contained too many words. This gift came from his heart for trustworthy, beautiful and informative programming.*

FCC approval of a new transmitter meant improved reach (power was boosted by almost 100 percent with a 1 million-watt digital broadcast signal) and quality, but it also meant a capital campaign correction — at least another $600,000 would be needed. The final stages of digital conversion were accomplished without a significant hitch on June 12, 2009, and Kuehl oversaw the shutdown of the analog transmitter. Now Channel 19 would have a split personality:

> *Channel 19.1 would broadcast high definition PBS national programs 24 hours a day; 19.2 would emphasize local and regional programs and offer "second chances" at popular programs such as "Nature" and "Nova"; 19.3 (Create) would broadcast such programs as "Lidia's Kansas City" around the clock; and 19.4 would disappear.*

After KCPT went digital, programs like "Nature" and "Nova" got more airtime.

LEHRER AND BERNANKE IN KC

Allan and Carol Hallquist hosted a reception at their Hyde Park home for Jim Lehrer on July 25, attended by major Channel 19 supporters. Lehrer and the "NewsHour" staff were in Kansas City for a July 26 town hall meeting with Federal Reserve Chairman Ben Bernanke. The program, taped for PBS at the new Kansas City Federal Reserve Bank Building, discussed the national economy with local participation and Lehrer as moderator. It was a significant promotional and development opportunity for KCPT, made available by Lehrer. In addition to the national exposure on PBS, there were mentions in *Business Week* and a *Wall Street Journal* blog, and *The Star*'s Barnhart wrote: "This is a coup for KCPT, the Kansas City public TV station that continues to outperform its 31st-largest-market stature."

In October, PBS' "Craft in America" featured Kansas City Art Institute faculty and alumni in one of the segments.

A documentary film, "The Next American Dream," chronicled the demise and rebirth of Kansas City's downtown as one example of the rejuvenation of American cities. Christopher Leinberger, a fellow at the Brookings Institution, was one of nine national urban land strategists and developers who provided input. He described some of his thinking about the program:

> *I have come to realize that our country is experiencing a fundamental change in how we build our metropolitan areas. This is affecting how we live, work and play, as well as introducing the next version of the American dream.*
>
> *"The Next American Dream" tells the story of how the Post World War II American dream led to the birth of the interstate highway system, suburbia, and an automobile-driven society. Today, a host of unintended consequences of that generation's choices — from environmental to social — is combining with a demographic shift in the number of households without children and an increasing demand for walkable urban spaces.*

The documentary was viewed across the country. KCPT, in partnership with the Kansas City Area Development Council, was key in the distribution process through PBS.

At the PT 19 annual meeting, Peter Yelorda, Blue Cross/Blue Shield executive vice president, was elected PT 19 chairman, succeeding Tracy Foster.

Clifford, the Big Red Dog, was at the Crown Center Ice Terrace on Feb. 27, 2010, for another KCPT "Kids on Ice."

April 2010 saw the end of a successful campaign that financed the new transmitter and the mobile studio.

In May, "Need to Know" replaced "Bill Moyers Journal." A PBS spokesman wrote: "'Need to Know' is indeed billed as a different program and Moyers especially is not exactly replaceable. Whether one loves or hates his program, he is a television icon who occupies a unique place in American broadcasting."

"Need to Know," produced by WNET in New York City, branded itself as a "TV and Web newsmagazine." By connecting and coordinating all news and public affairs content on-air and online, it would "break through the limitations of the broadcast schedule" and empower "audiences to 'tune in' anytime and anywhere."

In Washington, D.C., KCPT representatives accepted a Leadership Award from PBS in behalf of the Francis Family Foundation. The national award recognizes those who provide major public television funding. The foundation responded characteristically with grants to KCPT for "KCPT Reads" and for a proposed new series, "The Local Show."

With additional support from Jonathan Kemper and Commerce Bank, and with many positive comments, "The Local Show" launched July 15, 2010, and introduced viewers to local institutions and attractions. One show described the country's only official World War I Museum at the Liberty Memorial, for which it was awarded a regional Emmy. Another show was devoted to the acquisition and installation of "Ferment," an 18,000-pound, 56-foot-high, stainless-steel sculpture

"The Next American Dream" looked at Kansas City's downtown as an example of the rejuvenation of American cities.

In Kansas City for a town hall meeting, "NewsHour's" Jim Lehrer talked with KCPT supporters at a reception in his honor.

RICH SUGG/THE KANSAS CITY STAR

The revolutionary Bloch Building at the Nelson-Atkins Museum of Art.

The Local Show

"The Local Show" highlighted local attractions and institutions; more information was available online.

of a tree, planted near the Bloch Building at the Nelson-Atkins Museum of Art. It was outdoor sculpture on a monumental scale.

YES, WE YOUTUBE

"Local Show" viewers were invited to refer to a Web site (KCPT.org) for further information, and KCPT launched a YouTube channel. KCPT was continuing to progress as a telecommunications center.

Kansas City civic leader and philanthropist Henry Bloch and his wife, Marion, discovered and reported to me that they could watch the "Lawrence Welk Show" on KCPT at 5 p.m. Saturday and at 6 p.m. switch to Topeka's public TV station, KTWU, and enjoy the whole thing all over again.

Also in July, a special screening at Kansas City's Midland Theatre of the film "Freedom Riders" was timed to coincide with the national convention of the NAACP in Kansas City. Later, the program would air nationally as part of the "American Experience" series.

The hospital training program that used channels provided by KCPT was no longer using any of those ITFS frequencies previously acquired from PBS; all four were now excess capacity and available to lease to others for use in wireless telecommunication services. In August 2000, upon receipt of a $25,000 down payment, KCPT entered into a five-year lease of the frequencies to Sprint Communications Co. Before it expired, the lease was renegotiated by Bill Reed and Al Hallquist, and Sprint made a $500,000 down payment on another five-year term. At the end of that term, a new lease was negotiated with Sprint affiliate

RICH SUGG/THE KANSAS CITY STAR

One "Local Show" focused on the installation of "Ferment," a stainless steel sculpture of a tree "planted" near the Bloch Building.

Henry and Marion Bloch, here with their son Robert, were generous supporters of KCPT.

The KCPT production "Evicted, Foreclosed, Homeless" was an affecting look at the lives of homeless adults and children. A phone bank of counselors received 373 calls during the program.

Clearwire Spectrum Holdings, resulting in yet another up-front $500,000 payment in September 2010. These were enormous financial boons to KCPT.

KCPT's "Evicted, Foreclosed, Homeless" won a first-place award from the Missouri Broadcasters Association.

"Most people think [homelessness] is something that happens to somebody else, not me or among people who happen to look a certain way," said KCPT's executive producer of news and public affairs Nick Haines. The broadcast included intimate footage from Flip cameras given to adults and children willing to chronicle their experiences and share their stories. The documentary aired alongside a live discussion with community leaders and with a phone bank of trained counselors available to answer calls. That night, the phone bank received 373 calls.

At the September 2010 meeting, the board adopted some proposals for PT 19 board restructuring. As a result, chairmen would be elected for two-year terms. And at the annual meeting in October, Hunter Wolbach was elected chairman.

In anticipation of the 2010 national elections, KCPT scheduled a U.S. Senate debate for Oct. 14, 2010. This led to demands for access by Libertarian and Constitution Party candidates and two write-in candidates. The requests were rejected for failure to meet KCPT's criteria for debate participation, requiring a specified minimum level of public support. The station's policy, approved by the Federal Election Commission, is consistent with IRS and FCC regulations.

The annual meeting in October 2010 was the occasion for a very impressive education report on the current school year. In addition to ITV broadcasts, off-air services provided instruction for 53 school districts with 7,404 teachers, 97,592

(Continued on page 168)

PHOTOS: AARON LEIMKUEHLER/THE KANSAS CITY STAR

***THE GUTS OF THE OPERATION:* From top, the video control area at KCPT, from which cameras are monitored; automatic computers and servers in the master control room.**

From top, the audio room, where sound for local productions is controlled; set of "The Local Show." Background photo: Kevin Lambi in the studio control room.

THE GUTS OF THE OPERATION: Inset photos: Views of the audio console mixer. Background photo: The master control room at KCPT.

Intelli-Sat Recorder
SUNDANCE DIGITAL
Scheduled Events
Queued Events
Devices
DELL
DELL
panoramar
RM-2443W-HD
6301B
FLARE
M.FLARE
FULL
RELATIVE
MASTER PED
HEAD POWER
OPT
CABLE
CCU
PREVIEW
ALARM
RANGE

Perhaps best known for his collaborations with author Gertrude Stein, composer and music critic Virgil Thomson was born in Kansas City and spent many years living in Paris.

(Continued from page 165)

students and 204 buildings. One of these, Learn 360, was Internet or service-based and contained 26,600 video clips. School teachers and children could see the dark side of the moon, molecules combining or a difficult mathematical formula graphed in four dimensions.

All seven universities in KC REACHE had renewed, and St. Louis Community College and Butler Community College (Kansas) were new affiliate members. KCPT Reads had another paying customer: the University Academy kindergarten class joined, funded by the Friends of University Academy. But the funding was still largely philanthropic for a program that provided books monthly to nearly 2,000 underserved metropolitan area children.

Also in October, the National Science Teachers Association held its first science teachers' conference in Kansas City, with WGBH-Boston participating in the closing event with TV's Bill Nye the Science Guy.

A special "Check Please" show was produced because a young man with a terminal illness had expressed an interest in being on the program. Funders were plentiful.

KCPT was invited by WGBH-Boston to join a group of 10 PBS stations sharing their funding practices with the remainder of the Public Broadcasting System — recognition that KCPT's were among the best. The Boston station had received a $500,000 grant for the project.

JOE LEDFORD/THE KANSAS CITY STAR

Channel 19 filmed early and often in the new Kauffman Center for the Performing Arts. Above, the Kansas City Symphony performing in Helzberg Hall, part of the grand opening celebration.

There was a successful partnership with Kansas City's Union Station in connection with the Princess Diana exhibit at the station.

Another was a cooperative venture with Nonprofit Connect for joint use of the station's Community Room, which led to the nonprofit organization establishing a business office and training facility at the station and rental income for KCPT.

In his May-June 2011 *KC Studio* column, Kliff Kiehl announced that KCPT had its mobile studio. "This studio has been talked about for years and I am proud to say that the unit is up and running. The unit will bring arts, culture, public affairs and just plain entertainment into the homes of our viewers — many who would have no other means to see what our great city has to offer."

A commemorative concert in the spectacular Helzberg Hall in the new Kauffman Center for the Performing Arts was filmed by KCPT and Inland Sea Productions on Oct. 20. Billed as "Homecoming: An Evening with Virgil T.," it was a tribute to Kansas City's most illustrious classical composer, Virgil Thomson. Excerpts, incorporated in a biography of Thomson, were broadcast nationally on PBS. And in "Raising the Roof," a special edition of "The Local Show," KCPT's Randy Mason and Steph Suetos took viewers behind the scenes at the Kauffman Center, showing them a cathedral for the arts.

On Nov. 10, there was a roast of the "Ruckus" panel (the Ruckettes) at Californos in Kansas City's Westport area. On stage to be skewered were Gwen Grant, Woody Cozad, Mary O'Halloran and Yael Abouhalkah, along with the program's host, Mike Shanin. U.S. Rep. Emanuel Cleaver headlined an entertaining group of roasters, egged on by Nick Haines. The evening concluded with remarks from PT 19 chairman Hunter Wolbach.

Sometimes the Ruckettes roasted other people and sometimes they were roasted — in this case to raise money for the station.

The "Ruckus" panelists are (clockwise, from top left): veteran Kansas City broadcaster and host Mike Shanin, Kansas City Star columnist Yael Abouhalkah, lawyer and former Missouri Republican Party chairman Woody Cozad, Urban League of Greater Kansas City president and CEO Gwendolyn Grant, and former Iowa state representative and co-founder of the National Women's Political Caucus Mary O'Halloran.

BACK TO BIG BIRD

As Channel 19 reached age 50, "Sesame Street" began its 42nd season. Big Bird has become an institution. He has his own postage stamp and a star on the Hollywood Walk of Fame. And when the Library of Congress celebrated its 200th anniversary April 2, 2000, he was one of 81 recipients of its "Living Legend Award."

It is Big Bird that is famous, not his "inside man" Caroll Spinney. Spinney can walk along the street without recognition, and when "Sesame Street" was named Best Children's Show by the Television Hall of Fame, he and his wife trod the red-carpeted auditorium entrance in anonymity. As Spinney says in his book *The Wisdom of Big Bird:*

> *Big Bird's fame is a funny thing, because he's a fantasy figure. In a way, he's not even real. Yet he lives and is famous.*

A whole new cast of characters joined the giant canary over the years — Elmo, Grover, Oscar, Abby and many others including, of late, the excitable, inquisitive, orange monster Murray. They bring laughter and learning to children and parents, and it is comforting to know that this will continue despite competition from alternatives in a new world of electronic marvels.

In the early days, the Children's Television Workshop had a nonbroadcast division that published books and magazines and licensed toys. Rae Paige Schwarz, a friend who had a background in urban education at the Urban League Street Academy in East Harlem, got a job there. Rae used her teaching experience to good advantage editing television teachers' guides and later was editor-in-chief of the *Electric Company* and *Sesame Street* magazines. She enjoyed her association with puppeteer and Muppets creator Jim Henson and others, and wrote me:

> *It was a wonderful place to work. An extraordinary group of creative people. I was honored to be their friend and colleague … a magical place to be at an extraordinary time.*

Meanwhile, local affairs programming, named "most needed" in that early 1973 KCPT poll, is still very important to KCPT viewers, and the station has responded with significantly more quality production despite a smaller staff. In the process, the station has developed new partnerships that not only fund productions but also generate much needed revenue to replace declining state and corporate support.

People in a democracy can be entrusted to decide all-important matters for themselves when they are an informed citizenry. As Bill Moyers said in *The Washington Post* in 2005:

> *Public television is an open classroom for people who believe in lifelong learning.*

The author, Ed Matheny, Jr., has a moment with Big Bird at KCPT.

The "Ruckus" set.

THE STATED GOAL of KCPT, its officers, directors, and employees, is to be the constructive storyteller of the Midwest, with locally produced stories connected to the area's economy, its human capacity and quality of life. According to KCPT president and CEO Kliff Kuehl, staff and reporters will be added as needed to realize this goal with delivery by all manner of media on a daily or weekly basis as appropriate.

The current strategic plan addresses the funding needed to realize KCPT's goal, by expanding and diversifying sources of revenue, increasing major gifts and the number and size of membership and underwriting renewals, and growing the endowment fund.

Important focus areas: better connection with all of the diverse constituencies of KCPT, collaboration or even merger with other media organizations, alliances with Kansas City non-profit groups and more aggressive marketing.

As Kliff Kuehl puts it: "With the market failures we've seen in commercial print and television, the need is growing for a trusted place for the community to converse, collaborate and connect — an information source that brings more light than heat. Because of this need, public television has a long, bright future in Kansas City."

IN 2011, Channel 19 passed a golden milestone, its 50th anniversary.

KCPT is now well-positioned to serve its community in a PBS system of autonomous stations relying almost entirely on local support. Its loyal, talented employees provide informative, entertaining programs year after year.

Instructional television thrives — Big Bird lives. The value of ITV's broader educational contributions to viewers of all ages cannot be overstated.

"One man's meat is another man's poison." The 1709 English proverb has application to KCPT's public affairs telecasts and, quite often, national PBS productions. Responses to controversial programs have varied, depending largely on the viewer's personal taste and political orientation. Local control of programming as opposed to dependence upon national production centers has enabled KCPT to better reflect and respect the views and interests of its constituents.

KCPT has been quite important in the lives of a very large number of people, as evidenced by their expressions of appreciation or even their criticism, their financial and political support and volunteer participation.

Wallace Westfeldt, an old friend with impressive journalism credentials (Peabody Award, executive producer of the Huntley-Brinkley Report and NBC Nightly News, to mention a couple) asked me: "What is there about Kansas City that made it produce what is demonstrably one of the best public stations in the country?"

The following elements occur to me.

Essential were early recognition by Kansas City school superintendent James Hazlett of the value to the community of a public television station and the willingness of the Kansas City school board to put their baby up for adoption so that it might have a better future.

The founders of KCPT were respected community leaders whose participation gave credibility to a fledgling enterprise in a relatively new medium. They had little conception of the potential of their handiwork but they sensed that something was there that deserved to be explored and exploited, and proceeded without personal agendas.

The greater Kansas City community adopted the station with enthusiasm, appreciating the educational and entertainment value of Big Bird and the BBC, and enjoying the excitement of TV auctions and other opportunities to be part of "show biz" in a worthy cause. Here in the heart of America there was nothing comparable.

The early decision to cross the state line was no small achievement in "Border War" country, where State Line Road impeded community progress on many an occasion. The decision more than doubled Channel 19's potential market and led to the formation of one of the nation's largest instructional television programs.

The cooperation of Kansas City's commercial television stations has been unique and synergistic, to the great benefit of the community.

The fortuitous participation of John Masterman and Charles Gusewelle and the unwavering support of public television mainstays Jim Lehrer and Lidia Bastianich provided stature otherwise beyond the reach of a community station. (Masterman came to Kansas City from New York City in 1973 to anchor the news at NBC affiliate WDAF-TV and within two years joined Channel 19. KCPT's Bill Reed encountered Gusewelle and his Lena River project at a social gathering.)

Kansas City is notable for the generosity of its citizenry. Philanthropy, large and small, makes all the difference in the capacity of public television to accomplish its mission, and KCPT has had it in abundance...ranging from the menial to the millions.

Recognition of the importance of local focus dates back to the early days of KCPT and has only grown over the years. It is one of the great strengths of the station, which has also been in the vanguard of electronic evolution from broadcast to telecommunication center, and digital pioneering.

There is an esprit de corps, fomented by KCPT leadership, which attracts and retains remarkably talented employees who enjoy and take pride in their work:

> *I don't know how it's possible to get across that those of us who work here have not just devoted ourselves to the mission of the station but we have pulled our friends and family into the mix as well. I've been here for 16 years and when I started I thought this would be something I'd do for a couple of years.*
>
> *My best friend from home reminded me of how we used to write our own scripts for "Sesame Street" and act them out in the front yard for our parents. She gave me a Bert and Ernie doll set that I still have as a reminder of how at the young ages of 6 and 7, we were going to be working for PBS.*
>
> *I grew up in rural Iowa; I saw my first ballet on PBS, my first opera, my first lion attack, the list goes on. I marvel that 30 years later, we're still doing programming that makes a difference and it's pretty amazing to be part of it. And even more amazing to be a part of it here locally where we have the ability to see the people whose lives we change, even if in the slightest of ways.*
>
> *Not everything we do will move someone to volunteer at a soup kitchen or go out and vote, but every piece we do helps the people of this community appreciate the uniqueness of this city just a little bit more.*
>
> — *Angee Simmons, KCPT reporter and producer*

THE MANUSCRIPT for this book was written by pecking away on a word processor, but the author is much indebted to many persons for the end product.

Thanks to the considerable editorial skills of Carol Powers, *The Audacious Rise of KCPT: 20 Years of Daring Broadcasting at Kansas City's Public Television Station* reads less like a lawyer's pedantic work and offers a more lively and complete context of the time and place of events affecting KCPT. My daughter-in-law, the talented D.J. Hyde Matheny, designed a most attractive format (no nepotism... she was chosen by Doug Weaver, the publisher). Together, they collected and assembled quotes and pictures in a meaningful way. I enjoyed their sense of humor and appreciated their patience, which made our partnership in this enterprise most enjoyable for me.

Charles Gusewelle, a constant KCPT advocate, contributed the priceless Foreword to the book.

The Husch Blackwell law firm provided support services in the production of the manuscript, with a particular bow to library assistant Susan K. Osborn and legal administrative specialist Mary Stone.

The book as you see it would not have been possible without the ongoing professional assistance of *The Kansas City Star's* Derek Donovan, Eric Winkler and Jo Ann Groves. *Star* photographer Aaron Leimkuehler shot most of the contemporary pictures. The thought-provoking, if not always clairvoyant, quotations scattered throughout the book were gleaned from the fascinating and well-edited website Terra Media.

The manuscript was reviewed for accuracy and anecdotal additions by retired KCPT president and CEO William Reed and retired vice president of telecommunications and technology David Welsh. It was graciously supported by a host of current KCPT personnel including president and CEO Kliff Kuehl; chief development officer Michael Zeller; chief content officer Michael Murphy; executive producers Nick Haines and Randy Mason; producer/writers Angee Simmons and Pamela James; chief technology officer Jeff Evans; receptionist/writer/producer Sandy Woodson; director of leadership giving Michelle Thornton; and executive assistant Judith Ferguson.

Most of the photographs, letters and records in this book came from the archives of KCPT and *The Kansas City Star.*

Other photographs and anecdotes were furnished by Mary Davidson Cohen, George E. Powell III, Morton Sosland, Douglas Curran, Barnett Helzberg, David Francis, Jessica Brockmeier, Karen Rankin, Harvey Bodker and Tracy Droz Tragos.

EDWARD T. MATHENY, JR., KCPT's first president, was a history major at the University of Missouri, where he played varsity basketball and was elected to Phi Beta Kappa. A Navy veteran of World War II, he served on the staff of Fleet Admiral Chester Nimitz and also participated in the occupation of Japan. A *cum laude* graduate of Harvard Law School, he practiced law for more than 50 years.

He was chancellor of the Episcopal Diocese of West Missouri, president of Saint Luke's Hospital, a chairman of the Eye Foundation and served on various corporate and non-profit boards. The Edward T. Matheny Jr./Missouri Endowed Chair in Neuroscience was established in 1998 at St. Luke's Neuroscience Institute. He is a member of the Missouri Academy of Squires and this is his sixth history book on a subject of local interest.

The Emmy case at KCPT. Thirty and counting.

I believe television is going to be the test of the modern world.
In this new opportunity to see beyond the range of our vision
we shall either discover an unbearable disturbance
of the general peace or a saving radiance in the sky.
We shall stand or fall by television — of that I am sure.

— E. B. WHITE,
celebrated American essayist and writer,
in *The New Yorker,* 1938